Diary Method

Bloomsbury Research Methods

Edited by Graham Crow and Mark Elliot

The Bloomsbury Research Methods series provides authoritative introductions to a range of research methods which are at the forefront of developments in a range of disciplines.

Each volume sets out the key elements of the particular method and features examples of its application, drawing on a consistent structure across the whole series. Written in an accessible style by leading experts in the field, this series is an innovative pedagogical and research resource.

Also available in the series

Community Studies, Graham Crow

GIS, Nick Bearman

Inclusive Research, Melanie Nind

Qualitative Longitudinal Research, Bren Neale

Quantitative Longitudinal Data Analysis, Vernon Gayle and Paul Lambert

Rhythmanalysis, Dawn Lyon

Forthcoming in the series

Embodied Inquiry, Jennifer Leigh and Nicole Brown

Statistical Modelling in R, Kevin Ralston, Vernon Gayle, Roxanne Connelly and Chris Playford

Diary
Method

Research Methods

Ruth Bartlett and Christine Milligan

BLOOMSBURY ACADEMIC
LONDON • NEW YORK • OXFORD • NEW DELHI • SYDNEY

BLOOMSBURY ACADEMIC
Bloomsbury Publishing Plc
50 Bedford Square, London, WC1B 3DP, UK
1385 Broadway, New York, NY 10018, USA

BLOOMSBURY, BLOOMSBURY ACADEMIC and the Diana logo are trademarks
of Bloomsbury Publishing Plc

First published Open Access under a Creative Commons license in 2015 as *What is Diary Method?*,
this title is now also available as part of the Bloomsbury Research Methods series.
This edition published 2021

Series design by Charlotte James
Cover image © shuoshu / iStock

A catalogue record for this book is available from the British Library.

Library of Congress Cataloging-in-Publication Data

Names: Bartlett, Ruth, 1965- author. | Milligan, Christine, 1954- author.
Title: Diary method : research methods / Ruth Bartlett and Christine Milligan.
Other titles: What is diary method?
Description: [Revised edition]. | New York: Bloomsbury Academic, 2020. | Includes bibliographical
references and index.
Identifiers: LCCN 2020034894 (print) | LCCN 2020034895 (ebook) | ISBN 9781350187184 (hardback) |
ISBN 9781350187177 (paperback) | ISBN 9781350187191 (epub) | ISBN 9781350187207 (ebook)
Subjects: LCSH: Diaries–Therapeutic use. | Medical care–Research–Methodology. | Social sciences–
Research–Methodology. | Research–Methodology.
Classification: LCC RC489.D5 B37 2020 (print) | LCC RC489.D5 (ebook) | DDC 615.8/5163–dc23
LC record available at https://lccn.loc.gov/2020034894
LC ebook record available at https://lccn.loc.gov/2020034895

ISBN: HB: 978-1-3501-8718-4
PB: 978-1-3501-8717-7
ePDF: 978-1-3501-8720-7
eBook: 978-1-3501-8719-1

Series: Bloomsbury Research Methods

Typeset by Deanta Global Publishing Services, Chennai, India

To find out more about our authors and books visit www.bloomsbury.com
and sign up for our newsletters.

Contents

Series foreword

The idea behind this book series is a simple one: to provide concise and accessible introductions to frequently used research methods and of current issues in research methodology. Books in the series have been written by experts in their fields with a brief to write about their subject for a broad audience.

The series has been developed through a partnership between Bloomsbury and the UK's National Centre for Research Methods (NCRM). The original 'What is?' Research Methods Series sprang from the eponymous strand at NCRM's Research Methods Festivals.

This relaunched series reflects changes in the research landscape, embracing research methods innovation and interdisciplinarity. Methodological innovation is the order of the day, while still maintaining an emphasis on accessibility to a wide audience. The format allows researchers who are new to a field to gain an insight into its key features, while also providing a useful update on recent developments for people who have had some prior acquaintance with it. All readers should find it helpful to be taken through the discussion of key terms, the history of how the method or methodological issue has developed, and the assessment of the strengths and possible weaknesses of the approach through analysis of illustrative examples.

This book is devoted to diary method, which is an approach to analysing social life that has been used by researchers in the social sciences for a long time, but which is enjoying growing popularity as a result of both technological and social changes. As Ruth Bartlett and Christine Milligan show, contemporary researchers have been alive to the possibilities of new technologies being employed to capture people's behaviour and perceptions close to the points in time that they occur, and in a way that is convenient to research participants. The authenticity of the material collected through the use of the diary method is a further attraction of the approach for both participants and researchers, and this also helps to explain why this way of capturing the social world is marked by so much enthusiasm. Keeping a record of time use and timings can be a revelation to people who keep diaries as well as to researchers, and the purpose of charting the rhythms and routines in everyday life is readily apparent in a whole range of fields, including health behaviours and domestic life. Inevitably, of course, there are ethical as well as practical challenges to the use of an approach that tracks people's lives over time, and the potentially intrusive and time-consuming character of diary research means that it will not be appropriate for all areas of social scientific investigation. Nevertheless, the vibrancy of the field is nicely illustrated by the remarkable extent to which the book is able to draw upon recently published studies that have employed diary methods, and all the indications are that diaries will only grow in importance as part of the social scientist's toolkit.

The books cannot provide information about their subject matter down to a fine level of detail, but they will equip readers with a powerful sense of reasons why it deserves to be taken seriously and, it is hoped, with the enthusiasm to put that knowledge into practice.

1 The development of diary techniques for research

Introduction

Everyone understands the idea of a diary. We have all kept a diary for various reasons and in various ways. For some people it may simply be used as a reminder for appointments or events, detailing where they need to be and what they need to be doing at different times; others may keep a more detailed diary or personal account of what they are doing and perhaps what they were thinking and feeling at the time. Individuals often develop personal preferences, routines and systems for keeping a personal diary and choose to keep what they record private. Others may choose, or be invited, to publish their diary; think, for example, of the British journalist and political aide Alastair Campbell who has published three volumes of diaries about his time serving alongside the then Prime Minister, Tony Blair. For many people, there is something inherently absorbing about writing and/or reading someone else's personal diary.

In this book, we review and discuss how diary method has been used by researchers in the social and health sciences and suggest that technologies and modern forms of communication are transforming this method of data collection. Diary method has arguably been the 'poor relation' of the methodological family in qualitative research, compared, for example, to interviews. As Atkinson and Silverman (1997) pointed out some time ago, we live in an 'interview society' where the only route to 'truth' is thought to be through a face-to-face interview. One only has to consider the amount of research textbooks on qualitative interviewing, compared with what has been until now a single text on diary method (Alaszewski, 2006a). Or, the fact that several well-regarded and popular texts on mixed methods and qualitative research make very little, if any, reference to diary method (see, e.g., Bowling, 2014; Creswell, 2014; Flick, 2014). Yet, even a cursory search of the research literature published since 1990 reveals over 4,800 papers using diary method. Moreover, the method continues to provide researchers with a flexible tool for collecting rich data, especially in light of digital, web and social networking technologies. In this book, we therefore aim to clarify the role of diary method in the researchers' toolkit and illustrate through empirical examples the value and limitations of this method for eliciting information and engaging participants in research. In particular, we consider a range of structured, semi-structured and unstructured approaches to diary method; some of the practical issues in designing diary research; and how this method can be modified and used to enable participants to take part in a study and have control over the process of data collection.

A distinctive feature of this book is the consideration given to how and why the diary method is used and might be modified for children and for adults who are frail or physically, cognitively or intellectually impaired in some way. Rather than assuming capacity (like standard research texts) we will discuss the strengths (and limitations) of utilizing diary method to collect data from people who may experience problems in remembering, writing, talking, thinking clearly and using diary-keeping equipment, such as electronic diaries and cameras. We discuss the importance and implications of modifying the diary method in the context of emerging inclusive research methodologies and outline the ways in which researchers have adapted the method to enable the participation of different groups in research.

Another distinctive feature of this book is the consideration given to technologies and modern forms of communication. As other researchers in this series have noted, probably the most significant development in research methods in the past decade is the advancement of digital technologies (Wiles, 2012). Digital devices, weblogging and social media sites like Facebook facilitate and encourage people to maintain and share a personal record of their everyday lives, and the information is stored in a chronological order, as it is in a diary. The question as to whether this constitutes a form of diary keeping that researchers can use is often asked by students and will be discussed in Chapter 4. In this sense, the book fits well with the 'What is?' series, as we consider the value of diary method not only from a historical and present-day perspective, but also its future potential in the hyper-digital age.

Differences between unsolicited and solicited diaries

A key distinction to make before discussing diary method in any great depth, and in the context of social research, is between unsolicited and solicited diaries. Diaries which people choose to keep voluntarily are an example of an unsolicited diary: no one has asked the diarist to keep the diary. We have already mentioned Alastair Campbell's prowess in diary keeping, and many others in the political arena have maintained and published an unsolicited diary, including Galeazzo Cino (1903–1944), Foreign Minister of Fascist Italy, and Tony Benn (1925–2014), British Labour politician, to name just two. Some individuals seem to be natural diarists and committed to recording their lives for others to read.

Unsolicited diaries have been kept by men and women and have been published for centuries. *The Diaries of Samuel Pepys* (1633–1703) is perhaps one of the earliest and most well-known examples of an unsolicited diary, but there are countless other examples written by ordinary people, some of whom find themselves in extraordinary situations, which have been published. As well as the *Diary of Anne Frank*, there is *Dorothea's War*, which comprise the diaries of the First World War nurse Dorothea Crewdson; and the diaries of Martha Ballard (1785–1812), a midwife living in New England, have been researched and used by an historian to explore the community life and health care of post-revolutionary America (Ulrich, 1991). While these are fascinating accounts of everyday life, they are not the main focus of this book, which perhaps should be more accurately entitled: What is *solicited* diary method?

Solicited diaries are diaries that people have been asked to keep for a particular reason, notably for research purposes. This approach, in which a participant records his or her thoughts, feelings and/or behaviours under the direction of an individual researcher, has been part of the researcher's toolkit since the 1930s and is the main focus of this book. Perhaps one of the earliest and best examples of a traditional solicited diary is the Mass Observation Project (MOP), described below.

The Mass Observation Project (MOP) has been recording everyday life in the UK since 1937, when they called for people from all parts of the country to record everything they did from when they woke up in the morning to when they went to sleep at night on 12th May. This was the day of George VI's coronation. The resulting diaries provide a glimpse into the everyday lives of people across Britain and have become an invaluable resource for those researching countless aspects of the era.

The MOP was revived in 1981 and currently has a national panel of 500 volunteer participants who respond to 'Directives' or open-ended questions sent to them by post or email three times a year. The Directives contain two or three broad themes, which cover both personal issues and wider political and social issues and events, including, for example, the Scottish Referendum 2014 and Eurovision. Participants retain anonymity and therefore write openly and candidly. Researchers are invited to collaborate with MOP to help develop new directives.

This text and further information about MOP can be found on the website http://www.massobs.org.uk/mass_observation_project.html.

Another example of how and why a diary might be solicited to gain rich insights into a certain aspect of life can be seen in relation to the activities of think tanks. In May 2014, the Commission on the Future of the Home Care Workforce solicited a series of diaries from home care workers and published these on their website as a blog. The diary blogs provide an account of the home care workers' visits to people with high support needs and the range of challenges they encounter, notably a lack of time to engage with service users and talk to them about their care needs. An extract from one of the blogs is given below.

Monday

Well it was a struggle to get out of bed today, day 15 without a break. I have to work extra to be able to afford essential repairs to my car, without the car I am limited to the amount of work I can do and areas would need to be restricted meaning less money to live on. Yet there is no petrol allowance or consideration to the increase in my insurance.

My first call today is to assist a lady out of bed; it's a two person call as she is very disabled. When I arrived there was an awful smell, I then noticed that her commode had not been emptied the night before and had been placed right next to her bed, how she managed to sleep is a wonder! We have 1 hour to assist but once she is safely seated I left the other carer to assist with her breakfast and tidying up as my next call often takes much more time than is allocated.

This text and further information about the project can be found on the website http://www.lgiu.org.uk/2014/05/12/diary-of-a-home-care-worker-part-1/.

Each blog ends with the amount of miles the care worker has travelled and the total sum of unpaid travel and work time. These entries highlight the need for more investment into social care and reveal the value of solicited diary method for giving voice to a group of people who may go unheard, in this case, home care workers. However, while these provide useful examples of solicited diary method, these approaches are not the main focus of the book either. Rather, our focus is on how solicited diary method has been and could be used as part of an individual researcher's toolkit to collect data about a given phenomenon.

Solicited diaries as part of researcher's toolkit

Asking people to keep a regular record of their experiences can capture rich data on personal events, motives, feelings and beliefs in an unobtrusive way and over a period of time. Researchers who use diary method come from a wide range of disciplines, including health sciences, medicine, economics, sports science, human geography, transport planning, psychology and gerontology. As such, the method has evolved as a data collection tool over the years.

Today there are various forms of solicited diary, each one reflecting researchers' particular domain of interest and preference in terms of study design. Perhaps one of the most established forms of solicited diary is the time diary. This involves participants recording events at a specified time or between a particular time frame. Time diaries are favoured by researchers wishing to examine patterns of behaviour and draw some kind of comparison. For example, in one study, researchers invited 165 couples with children to fill out a separate time diary for two days – a typical work-day and non-workday for twenty-four hours. The time-diary technique allowed them to compare mothers' and fathers' reported involvement with childcare (Bureau, Services, & Science, 2005).

Another popular form of solicited diary is the travel diary. This is often used by transport planning researchers to elicit data regarding travel behaviour. Participants are typically asked to self-record the details of every journey they make on each occasion they can make it, so in effect the diary becomes an extended survey. This form of diary was used in the German Mobi*drive* study, which involved recruiting a total of 317 persons in 139 households to keep a six-week travel diary to investigate the rhythms of daily life and travel (Axhausen, Löchl, Schlich, Buhl, & Widmer, 2006).

Other forms of solicited diary have evolved within the health sciences to research health-related behaviours or bodily functions. For example, the 'food-diary method' has been used by researchers to investigate the eating and drinking patterns of healthy and diabetic subjects; this particular form of diary is so widely used it has become a validated measure, thus allowing for comparisons to be drawn between different nationalities (Bellisle, Dalix, & de Castro, 1999). Urinary diaries (micturition charts, frequency, volume and bladder diaries) provide another example of a particular form of solicited diary which has evolved; used in over sixteen studies, urinary diaries provide health researchers with useful numerical data (Bright, Drake, & Abrams, 2011). The development of different diary forms highlights the versatility of this method for collecting various sources of data, a point we return to in our discussion of study design in Chapter 2.

Although solicited diary method can be used on its own, it is perhaps more commonly used alongside other methods to investigate a research topic. The studies outlined below have all used diary method as part of a mixed methodology – that is, it has been used in combination with other methods, such as interviews and questionnaires, to provide a more detailed picture of the topic under investigation. Using a combination of data collection methods adds rigour, breadth, complexity, richness, depth and creativity to the research; plus it allows the limitations of one method to be offset with another (Bijoux & Myers, 2006).

Diaries and questionnaires were used to investigate the sexual behaviour of homosexual men Coxon (1999).

Audio diaries, photos and interviews were integrated in a study to explore the experiences of disabled young men transitioning to adulthood (Gibson, 2002).

Diaries and focus groups were used to explore the experiences of older people as customers of various public and private services (Koopman-Boyden & Richardson, 2013).

Daily diaries and weekly cognitive and affective assessments were used to determine the side effects of certain medications in people aged 65+ (Katz et al., 2005).

Diaries and semi-structured interviews were used by health researchers in a phenomenological study of midwives' experiences of intrapartum care (Bedwell, McGowan, & Lavender, 2012).

Written, photo, audio diaries and interviews were used to investigate the experiences of men and women with dementia who campaign for social change (Bartlett, 2012).

Diaries, interviews and self-directed photography were used by human geographers to understand movement through everyday spaces (Bijoux & Myers, 2006).

Audio diaries and pre- and post-season interviews were used to investigate young female athletes' ability to cope with stress (Tamminen & Holt, 2010).

Audio sleep diaries and interviews were used by sociologists to explore how children's sleeping patterns affect parents' sleep (Venn, Arber, Meadows, & Hislop, 2008).

It is apparent from the studies featured above that diaries are commonly combined with an interview. Often referred to as the diary-interview method (DIM), the technique involves a pre-diary interview and post-diary 'debriefing' interview, as well as the diary-keeping phase (Zimmerman & Wieder, 1977). One geographer who researched urban public culture using diary-interview method describes it like this: 'the diary becomes a kind of performance or reportage of the week, and the interview a recounting or reperformance' (Latham, 2003, p. 2002). Greater depth can be obtained by diary-interview method as participants have the opportunity to talk about diary entries and the researcher is able to explore in more depth the entries diarists have made.

Combining methods to collect data is a complex and challenging process, and it is beyond the remit of this short text to discuss mixed methodology in any great detail. Besides, there are several key texts on mixed methods for readers to access, most notably by John Creswell and the *What is Qualitative Research?* published in this series, which discusses some of the issues raised by the mixed methods movement (Hammersley, 2013). Nevertheless, it is helpful to identify and reflect on the ways in which researchers have used diary method alongside other data collection techniques; thus some of the specific issues that arise in combining diary method with other approaches are picked up and discussed in Chapter 2.

What insights are provided through diary method as a data source?

So what is the appeal of diary method? Why do so many researchers choose to integrate this approach into their study design? First and foremost, diary method is favoured by researchers for 'capturing life as it is lived' (Bolger, Davis, & Rafaeli, 2003). Rather than someone recounting an event or feeling (as is the case with a qualitative interview), diary method allows the participant to record it as it occurs (or at least closer to the moment that it occurs). This is thought to reduce recall bias, a point we return to in several places in this book.

Not only does diary method allow participants to record events as and when they occur, but the method allows for an extended period of data collection. Participants are typically asked to maintain a diary over a certain number of weeks, sometimes months, depending on the phenomenon under investigation. In one diary-interview-based study on athlete stressors and coping strategies, for example, it made sense for the sixteen adolescent basketball players to complete pre- and post-season interviews and maintain an audio diary across the three phases of the season (early, mid and late) (Tamminen & Holt, 2010). Being able to gather data for a longer period of time is important when seeking to understand the daily rhythms of everyday life, or if you wish to study changes within a person, such as coping strategies, as was the case with the athlete study. As such, the micro-level data provided through diary techniques can shed valuable light on areas of a participant's life that one would not otherwise be able to access, as outlined below.

Within-person variation and effects. Diary method is ideal for capturing data about changes within a person, because the reporting period is extended with a diary. For example, Cleveland & Harris (2010) used written diaries to investigate young people's substance misuse cravings over time. In another study, participants were asked to keep a crying and mood diary ranging in days between 40 and 73 (Bylsma, Croon, Vingerhoets, & Rottenberg, 2011). Also, the effects of daily stressors, such as commuting between home and work, caring for others and problems with technology, are processes that occur within the individual that has been captured through diary method (Seltzer et al., 2010).

Greater reporting of sensitive or otherwise 'unseen' behaviours. Several researchers report on the value of using diary method to research sensitive behaviours such as sexual activity and sexuality. In fact, so many researchers use diary method to research this topic area, and a handbook has been published on conducting human sexuality research using diary method (Okami, 2002). Sleep is another aspect of life that is researched using diary method, particularly audio diaries, because the method lends itself to eliciting what sleep researchers have called 'narratives of the night' (Hislop, Arber, Meadows, & Venn, 2005).

Unique insights about the body and creative practices. Information about how someone looks, speaks, behaves and touches can all be gained through diary method, particularly, visual, audio and/or photo diaries. For instance, video and audio diaries can make the body 'knowable' because they make known how a participant moves and sounds (Bates, 2013), and photo diaries can reveal the importance of touch as a homemaking practice (Morrison, 2012). A leading proponent of sensory methods describes the data elicited through video and audio diaries as performative and dynamic (Pink, 2007).

Having identified the particular insights gained through diary method, it is possible to summarize the main topic areas that have been researched using diary method; these are:

- Eating and drinking habits
- Sleeping patterns
- Sexual activity
- Travel behaviour
- Sports and sports coaching
- Living with a disability, ill health or long-term condition
- The practices and attitudes of health-care workers
- Use of physical space and interactions with the built environment
- Daily stressors and coping strategies

The list of topics is not exhaustive; a diverse range of topics have been explored using solicited diary method, as we have already mentioned, and it is an extremely versatile and widely used data collection tool.

Researching this book

This book aims to provide an up-to-date, accessible and complete account of diary method in the context of social science research. It is based on a comprehensive review of the research literature; key databases were searched for research studies that have used diary method and a further 'sweep' for evidence was conducted using Google scholar to identify all published literature in English regarding solicited diaries. If a paper or document featured the term 'diary method' or a derivative thereof – for example, 'e-diary' or 'diary-interview method'– in the title and/or abstract, it was downloaded, stored onto a reference manager and organized according to the chapter themes. Given the emphasis in this series on the social sciences, we concentrated on those studies that have used diary method in cognate fields and filtered out those from other disciplines such as computer science and engineering. Many of the social science–related studies we identified are cited and described in this text. As such, the book functions as a useful and comprehensive reference point for researchers considering using diary method in their project.

In terms of the structure of the book, having provided a brief overview of diary method in this introductory chapter, we move on in Chapter 2 to discuss the process of engaging with diary techniques in more depth. This chapter covers the theoretical and epistemological underpinnings of diary method and outlines the type of research questions best addressed through solicited diary method. In Chapter 3, we focus on the practical aspects of designing a diary study and analysing diary data, including audiovisual data. Close attention is paid in this chapter to the analysis and interpretation of diary data and we discuss aspects of this method most likely to be of concern to researchers, including, for example, how to ensure rigour, validity and reliability and trustworthiness of findings. Chapter 4 engages with the digital age and explains how new technologies and electronic devices are changing the nature of diary method. Chapter 5 turns to issues of empowerment, control and ethics, and appraises the strengths and limitations of diary method in the context of participatory research and building equitable relations. Finally, in Chapter 6 we conclude by outlining the strengths and limitations of this method before suggesting there is a shifting practice in diary keeping from traditional low-tech to hi-tech contemporary method (from pen to pen-drive!).

2 Engaging with diary techniques

Introduction

In this chapter we discuss not just the use of solicited diary techniques in research but also the different ways of designing, collecting and using diary data and the different forms and purposes to which it can be attached. We distinguish between the use of simpler and more complex structured and unstructured (quantitative and qualitative) designs, explaining how and why researchers can use this method in different ways. In doing so, we consider the questions researchers need to pose before engaging with diary techniques and the contribution that these approaches can bring to the study of different questions, phenomena and social problems. We illustrate this through reviewing a sample of studies from health and social research that have taken different approaches to the design and implementation of diary method. Here, the chapter outlines the areas of everyday life and the nature of data that are typically collected from structured approaches, including, for example, sleep patterns, food intake and alcohol consumption. It also draws on a range of studies that take an unstructured approach, highlighting the different types of data that can be gathered using this approach to diary method. We include day-to-day accounts of particular experiences over time, such as campaigning, caregiving and living with disability. Practical issues, such as how diary method is combined with other research techniques such as interviews and visual methods, will also be discussed. The chapter concludes with a discussion of the use of audio and photo diaries in the context of sensory methodology.

Why use diary methods?

As noted in the introduction, solicited diaries form part of a research process in which selected informants actively participate in both recording and reflecting on their own actions, experiences and behaviours.

As such, they can prove useful for not only capturing the weight and meaning people attach to different events, issues and activities in their lives, but can create a record of their everyday actions and worlds. Solicited diary techniques have been used successfully with a wide range of participants including children, adolescents, disabled youth, people from ethnic minority groups, people with specific health-related problems, older people and people with dementia (see, e.g., Bartlett, 2012; Buchwald, 2009; Edinburgh, Garcia, & Saewyc, 2013; Gibson, 1995). The range of topics explored using diary techniques is similarly diverse and has been used to explore such topics as the relationship between body satisfaction and sexual experience (Zhaoyang & Cooper, 2013); influences on household demand for malaria treatment in resource-poor countries (Wiseman, Conteh, & Matovu, 2005); children's understanding of sustainable development (Walshe, 2013) and age differences in media multitasking (Voorveld & van der Goot, 2013), to name but a few. As these cases illustrate, diary studies are suitable for use with a wide range of participant groups including those that are often defined as 'vulnerable'. There is often an assumption – erroneously, as these studies infer – that such complex or time-consuming techniques are either inappropriate or will 'not work' for some groups of people. We discuss the issue of vulnerability in more detail in Chapter 5.

Whatever the topic or target group, the function of solicited diaries within a research project needs to be clarified at the outset, as the structure of the diary will vary accordingly (Nicholl, 2010). For instance, if the function of the diary is to gain an accurate record of how many times a participant engages in a particular activity over a specified time period, when and/or for how long, then a structured diary may be most appropriate. Here, the purpose of the diary is to gather numerical data that may then be analysed quantitatively. The strength of this type of approach to diary recording is that where accuracy is important, it can help to overcome problems of recall bias that can distort the recording of numerical data that are gathered at a single point in time – some time after the event occurs (as, for example, with a retrospective survey). This approach to diary keeping can also be used to facilitate the regular recording of validated measures of health and well-being over time. In the absence of any contextual data, the accuracy of structured diary recording can be supplemented by introducing visual elements to the diary. This approach is one that has long been used in studies of diet and nutrition. For instance, some researchers use photographic evidence to provide a visual record of portion size that can otherwise be rendered inaccurate by subjective assessment when recording dietary intake (Lanigan, Wells, Lawson, & Lucas, 2001). Others design this kind of diary study in ways that allow for the gathering of some qualitative data recording to help contextualize or qualify the quantitative recording.

Where the purpose of the diary is to provide access to a more in-depth understanding of people's interpretations of their worlds, semi- or unstructured diary recording techniques may be more appropriate as they can provide a useful tool for developing realistic pictures and sensitive descriptions of an individual's everyday life (Milligan, Bingley, & Gatrell, 2005). The detail gained in this type of recording can often be lost in face-to-face responsive mode methods such as interviews and focus groups where the respondent forgets the detail, recounts it inaccurately or takes the view that certain activities, events or experiences are too mundane to be worth recounting to the researcher (Nicholl, 2010). Moreover, diary method allows for the collection of naturalistic data – that is, information gathered 'in the moment' and in a 'real environment', like a home or the outdoors, rather than a research clinic or laboratory.

The distance between the researcher and diarist in this approach – where the researcher is removed from the setting in which the diary is completed – can also enable the diarist to feel more empowered in terms of what they choose to write and how they choose to write it. The distance between researcher and researched can also result in diarists feeling less 'judged' by their responses or less pressured into giving what they feel (rightly or wrongly) is the 'right' answer. Meth (2003) pointed to further potential benefits of a qualitative approach to diary keeping; in her study of the experiences of violence amongst women in South Africa, not only did she demonstrate its potential for researching highly sensitive topics that may be more difficult to broach using face-to-face methods, but she pointed to their potential to provide a therapeutic or cathartic experience. As one of her respondents wrote, *'Writing the diary was a task I liked to do....I also felt relieved. It was like a big luggage had been removed from my shoulders'* (p. 201). The potential benefits of diary keeping for the research participant will be explored in more detail in Chapter 5.

Whatever form of structure they take, Alaszewski (2006a) has pointed to four defining characteristics of the solicited diary as method that differentiates it from other methodological techniques:

1. They are defined by *regularity* – in that they are organized around a series of regular dated entries over a period of time.
2. They are *private* – that is, diaries are constructed by a specified identifiable individual who controls access to the diary during completion. While he or she may permit others to access the diary, failure to destroy the diary upon completion equates to tacit acceptance that others will access it (at least within the limitations of the informed consent given).
3. Diaries are *contemporaneous*, in that they are recorded at the same time or very close to the time when events or activities occur so do not suffer the limitations of recall bias in some other methods.
4. Diaries are a *time-structured record* that may be written (by hand or electronically), audio-recorded or visual – or a mix of any, or all, of these options. Entries consist of what the individual diarist considers to be relevant and important, including interactions, events, experiences, activities, thoughts and feelings.

These characteristics mean that as a research instrument, the solicited diary can provide a valuable tool for collecting detailed, chronologically structured, information about behaviour, events and other aspects of individuals' daily lives over a defined period of time.

In discussing the design of a structured diary-based study, it is helpful to consider the frequency of measurement points. The simplest diary designs require participants to make just one entry a day, often in the evening. More complicated designs require participants to make an entry several times a day. In both cases, researchers may choose to use interval-based sampling (at fixed times); event-based sampling (reporting when certain things occur, such as an asthma attack or episode of incontinence); or signal-based sampling (reporting when signalled by a text message or email, for example) (Rönkä, Malinen, Kinnunen, Tolvanen, & Lämsä, 2010). Below are some examples of how each of these strategies has been used within solicited diary studies. These examples highlight how the frequency of diary entries is an important decision to be made in diary design.

(a) **A combination of interval- and event-based sampling** was used in a diary study by Rönkä et al. (2010) to investigate family life. Over the course of one week, participants made a diary entry three times a day at fixed times (the interval) using mobile phone technology; entries were related to work and domestic stressors (the event).

(b) **Signal-based sampling** was used in the following studies to explore:

    (i)   pain in children aged eight years and over – here, participants responded to a text message (the signal) six times a day for around one week (Alfvén, 2010);

    (ii) what people do on the web – here, participants were sent an email (the signal) five times a day over a period of three days for a total of fifteen reminders (Kim & Jean, 2009).

    (iii) pubic hair removal – here, participants received a daily email reminder (the signal) to complete an online diary questionnaire about sexual activities that occurred alone or with a partner (Herbenick et al., 2013).

(c) **Event-based sampling** was used in an audio-diary study by Williamson, Leeming, Lyttle, & Johnson (2012) involving first-time mothers with breastfeeding difficulties. Participants were asked to make daily entries twice after a feeding session (the event).

From structured to unstructured approaches in solicited diary methods

While inevitably diaries are solicited with a certain agenda in mind, the precise form of the diary, and how data are recorded within it, will differ depending on the aim and purpose of the study it is contributing to. As we have previously noted, diaries can be used as a single source of data or as part of a multi-method research design that may incorporate elements ranging from structured to semi-structured and unstructured or a mix of methods. Its form and approach can thus range across a spectrum from the written structured diary recording through to the written unstructured and visual diary approaches and various combinations of these approaches in between. Each of these variations has an important, but distinct, role to play in the social researcher's toolbox.

Structured approaches to diary keeping

Structured diary keeping adopts a checklist or other fixed-response format that is designed to record and gather numerical data on how often
a diarist undertakes a specific action or activity. The diarist is generally
required to regularly 'log' items against a list of predefined actions or
validated measures over a predefined period of time. This structured
approach to solicited diary recording has been used for over ninety years
but it has only been named as such by social scientists and health-related
researchers since the 1970s (Waldron & Eyer, 1975).

Perhaps the earliest example of a structured approach to diary keeping was conducted in 1913 by the Fabian Women's Group, who sampled
forty-two families living on a low income in a particular area of London
(Reeves, 1913). Although the term 'diary' is not used in this historical
account of an investigation into the relationship between family income,
mother's nutrition and infant health, it is clear from the approach taken
that that was the method used to collect data:

> It was found to be necessary, in order to secure the success of the
> investigation to inaugurate a system of accurate accounts. In no case
> were these accounts already in being, and it was therefore the task
> of the visitors to teach each woman in turn to keep a record of her
> expenditure for the week (Reeves, 1913, p. 11).

The women were asked to keep a record of all the money they received
from their husbands, all the money they spent and the items they spent
the money on, especially in respect of food. The author describes how
some of the women were better at sums than writing words and so the
visitor (researcher) faced some challenges ensuring the accuracy of data,
including, for example, double-checking figures and accounts with the
women. It is also noteworthy that eight of the women in the sample could
not read or write and therefore asked their husbands or an eldest child to
keep the record – thus, highlighting one of the limitations of the traditional pen-and-paper diary method: it relies on literacy skills.

In another early example of a structured approach to diary keeping, participants (all of whom lived in the same Austrian village) were
asked to complete meal records for one week and time sheets for a
single day outlining the way they spent their day (Jahoda, Lazarsfeld,
& Zeisel, 1972). The research was about the effects of unemployment

on men and their families and researchers wanted to 'find procedures which would combine the use of numerical data with immersion into the situation' (p. 1). Meal records and time sheets were just two of the tools they used, as data were elicited using a range of methods, including participant observation and documentary analysis, but the information gained through these records allowed the researchers to draw conclusions about peoples' use of time when unemployed. *Marienthal: The sociography of an unemployed community* has become a classic study and paved the way for the development of time-use diaries as a field of methodological study and enquiry.

Indeed, a more recent example of using a structured approach to diary keeping is from the now well-established field of time-use research. The specially structured diaries used in time-use surveys are regarded as a particularly effective method for establishing how people live their lives (Gershuny, 2000). The method is considered so effective that it has been deployed in multinational longitudinal studies to compare how people in different countries use time. Using diaries in this way shows the potential of a structured approach for collecting data that could inform policymaking and decision-making at national and global levels.[1]

As well as time-diary techniques, work on emotional health and the impact of positive versus negative social exchanges typifies the rationale for, and use of, structured diary recording techniques within health research (Rook, 2010). This approach, Rook maintained, reduces respondent burden and ensures the capture of theoretically relevant data that can be analysed and replicated using statistical techniques. Following an initial interview, Rook's participants were asked to complete daily diaries composed of a set of fixed-response questions for a two-week period to assess the diarists' mood and any positive or negative social exchanges they may have experienced that day. The objective of the diary element of the study was to enable the researcher to assess the impact of social exchanges on the emotional well-being of her participants over time and to assess the potential predictive relationship of these exchanges to loneliness and social isolation. This structured approach to diary recording has been used to gather data on such diverse topics as instrumental activities of daily life amongst older people (Fricke & Unsworth, 2001), exercise adherence, marital interaction and relationship satisfaction (Feeney, 2002; Papp, Goeke-Morey, & Cummings, 2007); disabling and recurrent pain in children (Alfvén, 2010) and substance use and sexual risk-taking in

HIV-positive men (Boone, Cook, & Wilson, 2013). See below for a detailed overview of the structured approach taken in two of these studies.

Boone et al. (2013) used longitudinal diary method to examine the relationship between substance use and unprotected anal sex in a sample of 158 HIV-positive, mostly ethnic minority, men who have sex with men. Participants completed an internet-based structured weekly sex diary for six weeks. The men were asked to complete a survey each week on the same day, with a grace period of three days. The structured diary asked participants to provide details about their sexual behaviour and substance use in the past week (e.g. How many times have you used solvents in the past seven days? How many times have you engaged in sexual intercourse in the past seven days?).

Feeney (2002) used a structured approach to diary method to explore the link between spouse behaviour, marital satisfaction and emotional attachment. One hundred and ninety-three married couples were recruited to the project. Each participant was asked to complete a diary booklet containing two sets of records to be filled out on two consecutive days, one during the week and one during the weekend. Each record required the participant to note the number of hours spent in the presence of the spouse, to read through a checklist of ninety-five spouse behaviours and check all those that had occurred during the day and, finally, to rate the day on a Likert scale (1–9) relaying overall subjective satisfaction with the relationship.

A particular variant of the structured approach to diary method is the calendar or time-diary approach (Bellisle et al., 1999). Here the focus is on understanding behavioural mechanisms using time-space budgets across defined periods of time. Anastario and Schmalzbauer (2008) used time-space diaries in a study with Honduran migrants in the United States. Here, diarists were asked to record their activity – against a predefined set of categories – at thirty-minute intervals across a twenty-four-hour day for seven days. Data on the previous twenty-four-hour activity were collected by the researcher at exactly the same time each day in order to ensure a concrete point of reference with regard to the start and end time of the twenty-four-hour period, in order to ensure data accuracy and to minimize any inaccuracy in recall. In conjunction with ethnographic data, the diaries helped to elucidate factors that may be contributing to gendered disparities in health outcomes related to mobility amongst these Honduran migrants.

Semi- and unstructured approaches to diary keeping

In-depth semi- and unstructured diary recording is designed to encourage the diarist to write a more detailed temporal narrative, often around a loosely structured set of themes devised by the researcher. This is designed to gain a deeper understanding of a person's actions, experiences, thoughts and emotion around a particular topic. Those diaries designed to facilitate semi- or unstructured responses often allow space for diarists to record their own priorities, and in some instances may include scope for visual data to support the written accounts. Qualitative approaches to diary recording can thus prove useful for capturing the meaning and weight respondents attach to different events and experiences in their lives (Milligan et al., 2005). This can then be used as data in itself and/or used as a prompt to explore key time-related or other issues in more depth in follow-on interviews, as in the study by Orban, Edberg, and Erlandsson (2012) described below.

Orban and colleagues were interested in how the patterns of occupation of working women (aged between thirty and fifty) in two-parent families changed over time and the causes that lay behind those changes. To do so, they used semi-structured solicited time-geographical diaries combined with stimulated recall interviews. Participants were asked to complete twenty-four-hour diaries over a typical weekday twice, with an interval of ten weeks in between each twenty-four-hour diary completion. The diary was used as a self-report instrument in which the participant was asked to make notes about all activities undertaken during the twenty-four-hour period. In order to capture the participants' own perspectives, the time-geographical diaries were open format; however, instructions for completion and headings were included to ensure the following were updated during the completion of the diary:

- What occupation was being performed
- Time of changing occupation

- Where the participant was
- Who the participant was with
- State of mind during the occupation.

Upon completion of the twenty-four-hour diary, participants were asked to rate on a five-point scale how well the day typified an average day in their lives.

The diary data were then coded and converted into graphs illustrating the sequencing of occupations performed over the time period, how it was performed, the places it was performed in and the social networks involved. The graphs were then used as visual aids in open interviews to encourage participants to reflect on what they had done, how, why and who was involved. The diary facilitated an understanding of the complexity of these working women's daily lives, how their daily lives are always in a state of change and how their occupational performance is influenced by their physical and social environments.

Most structured or semi-structured diaries draw on the written word – whether recorded as hand-written accounts or (increasingly) submitted electronically as the technology becomes more affordable and widely available. However, reliance on written diaries can prove exclusionary to those whose writing skills are impaired, for example, due to illiteracy, age, disability or sight impairment, disorder of written expression or where detailed written expression may be difficult when it is not the diarist's first language. It is here that oral, audio-recorded diaries can play a useful role. Indeed, Worth (2009) notes that on a practical level the ease of operation of the recorder can make it particularly suitable for those with physical functional limitations. For those with access to computing facilities, low cost or freely available apps now make it possible to audio record (or even record audio-visually) directly onto a computer or laptop that can then be downloaded by, or for, the researcher or encrypted and sent electronically. Monrouxe (2009) has further suggested that audio-recorded diaries may have an advantage over the written word in that it allows the researcher to capture those subtleties of tone not captured in a written account.

Using sensory and audiovisual approaches to diary recording

There is a growing interest within the qualitative research community in sensory methodologies – a relatively new approach in which the researcher seeks to capture and engage with every aspect of the human experience, not just that which is reducible to language.[2] With this approach, it is important to find ways of eliciting data about a person's whole embodied experience, as well as finding out what a person thinks or feels about something. Bates (2013) took a sensory approach in her video-diary study exploring health and illness; participants with various health conditions were interviewed and then asked to complete a video diary for one month to 'show and tell the researcher about their body and condition' (p. 30). The video footage complemented the interview data, enabling the researcher to gain a fuller picture of people's lives and embodied experiences of living with ill-health.

A sensory approach to diary recording draws on audiovisual techniques such as filming, photography and self-recorded audio materials: methods that facilitate understanding of embodied or social and identity practices in the making. Such techniques can strengthen a diary study because they make the body visible and audible and allow the researcher to gain a more intimate and dynamic understanding of a person's life that is not possible through an interview alone. The value and power of such an approach to health researchers has been summarized by Rich and Patashnick (2002, p. 249):

> Other forms of data cannot duplicate the audio-visual record of four minutes of a girl coughing, wheezing and gasping for breath as she is increasingly overwhelmed by an asthma exacerbation or the disappointment in the face of a young man with spina bifida as he explains that he will not be able to pursue his lifelong dream of going to a culinary institute because the training kitchens cannot accommodate his wheelchair.

Another research team, who used both interview and photo-diary methods to explore child labour in the UK, found that the images child participants took added a significant dimension to their understanding:

Take the case of John, a 12-year-old boy living in an area of South Wales that had experienced massive de-industrialization over the previous 20 years. John had been a conscientious research participant, explaining diligently the detail of his work on the family sheep farm. From these accounts we knew the routines of his work, his developing animal husbandry skills and the pride he took in his growing dexterity with agricultural machinery. But it was only on seeing his photographs of tractors, a quad bike, workshops and farm buildings, fields and hillsides dotted with sheep some way off in the distance, that the scale of both the farm and John's endeavours became more fully apparent (Mizen, 2005, p. 130).

Others have emphasized how audiovisual data provides a unique window to people's embodied experiences. In the video-diary study by Bates (2013), for example, the video diaries 'created a space within which bodies could be seen, heard and felt' (p. 34). Similarly, in Gibson's study of disabled young men transitioning to adulthood, the researcher integrated audio and photo diaries with interviews to gain a 'mosaic of accounts and practices' (Gibson, 2002, p. 12). Researchers use sensory approaches, then, in a relatively unstructured way to complement textual diary data and to enrich understanding of the topic under investigation.

As well as enriching understanding, sensory and audiovisual approaches are particularly useful where literacy, capacity or memory recall may prove potential barriers to participation. Being able to film or photograph something enables individuals to express themselves in a freer way that is less reliant on language skills. This is perhaps why audiovisual methods have become increasingly popular in diary research involving young children (Buchwald, 2009; Edinburgh et al., 2013), people with physical disabilities (Gibson, 2002; Worth, 2009), learning disabilities (Aldridge, 2007) and adults with dementia (Bartlett, 2012). In particular, video-diary method is a well-established technique in children's research as it is considered useful for equalizing the power balance in the research encounter between child and adult researcher for addressing potential limitations of verbal expression amongst some children, as well as any potential limited concentration span (Buchwald, 2009). Sensory and audiovisual methods are, thus, useful for addressing potential exclusionary features of written diaries and help to develop equitable relations between the researcher and participants. We discuss this in more detail in Chapter 5.

Another methodological strength of sensory methods, and a reason why they differ from written diaries, is an epistemological one. Audio and visual techniques open up a whole new route to knowing the world – one which individuals are arguably already attuned with. As Latham (2003) contends, much of what individuals know, they learn tacitly and while this learning is not entirely subconscious it conforms to an internalized logic that is 'not ordered through the discursive' (p. 2005). In other words, non-discursive (visual) methods can prove invaluable for investigating this logic without expecting individuals to fully explain or articulate these practices through the written or spoken word. Rather, people can reveal their experiences, emotions, practices and identities through the recording of time-sequenced diary data by using either video or photographic recording. In sum, sensory methods are a useful design feature in diary studies, which can aid understanding and enable participation.

Mixed methods approaches

While diary techniques can be used as the sole and primary source of research data, as we have alluded to above, they can also be used as part of a mixed methods study. That is, they can be used as a precursor, an adjunct to or a follow-up to a survey, interview, observation or some other methodological technique. Latham (2003), for example, in his concern to articulate an understanding of the everyday inhabitation of public spaces and urban public culture as embodied practice drew on the diary-interview method (DIM) and diary-photograph, diary-interview method (DPDIM), pioneered by Zimmerman and Wieder in the 1970s. Here, the diarist acts as a proxy observer, whose 'observations' are then followed up in an in-depth interview with the researcher. In Latham's case, the diarist was additionally supplied with a camera and encouraged to include photographs of significant events, places and actions alongside the written narrative in a weekly diary. In this context, as with the Orban et al. (2012) study referred to earlier, the role of the diary becomes either that of a precursor and aide memoir to stimulate discussion in subsequent interviews or, significantly, that the subsequent interview can serve the purpose of testing the plausibility and robustness of the diary account. Latham (2003), however, suggests that as a methodological technique the diary can serve an additional purpose in that it:

becomes a form of performance or reportage of the week and the interview a re-accounting, or re-performance. Thus rather than seeing the idiosyncrasies of individual diarists as a problem, the methodological focus shifts into plugging into (and enabling) respondents' existing narrative resources (p. 2002).

Gibson (2002) used a mix of qualitative methods, including audio diaries combined with visual photographic data supplemented by interviews to gain a deeper understanding of disabled young men's experiences of transitioning to adulthood. The researcher was keen to understand the intersectionality of gender, disability and life-stage identities. Using this combination of techniques enabled the researcher to capture identity practices, engage disabled male youth, encourage reflection and provide some independence in data generation in ways that facilitated their understanding of how disabled young men establish, maintain and reform their identities in everyday practices. The photo and diary opportunities they maintained provided participants with the time, space and impetus to reflect on and later share their transitioning experiences.

But mixed methods approaches to diary recording can also involve the development of diaries that are themselves designed to gather both structured and unstructured data over a defined period of time. As suggested earlier, this approach can be particularly useful where the accuracy of numerical recording of predefined items may be rendered more accurate through the addition of visual data, or where the integration of more in-depth semi- or unstructured data alongside structured diary recording enables the diarist to contextualize or qualify his or her structured responses. This, in turn, can aid the researcher in a more accurate interpretation of the structured responses.

Engaging with diary techniques – what are the questions to consider?

In this final section, we summarize some of the key questions to consider when designing and applying solicited diaries as a form of data collection. Ensuring solicited diary method is appropriate for addressing your research as either the sole method of data collection or part of a wider study design is an important decision, for while a well-designed solicited diary can yield significant insights into an individuals' actions or experiences over time that may not be so accurately gained using other research techniques. By the same token, a badly designed and implemented diary study may involve considerable effort, but yield little useful information. Not only do you need to consider whether solicited diaries can yield insights that help to address the key aims and objectives of your study in ways that are more insightful than other forms of data collection, but you need to decide whether this technique is most useful as a stand-alone method, or as part of a mixed methods design.

You also need to think carefully about how long you need to gather the data for, whether particular times of the year, week, days are important to the study and whether the temporal narrative is a key element of your study. What are the risks in undertaking longitudinal solicited diary studies and how will you mitigate these risks? Related to this, it is important to consider whether you wish, or need, to collect data in a highly structured format at very specific time intervals. Alternatively, are you aiming to gather chronological data, but data that seek to understand experiences or events in the participants' own words? Drawing on and adapting the work of Nicholl (2010), we have developed a set of core questions that are important to consider before engaging with diary techniques in your research design.

Table 2.1 Fourteen questions to consider before engaging with diary techniques

1.	Is the tool appropriate for your research questions and aims?
2.	Will the diary be used on its own or as part of a mixed methods design?
3.	Is its purpose to inform or confirm other data?
4.	Are you using diary method to collect structured, semi- or unstructured data, or a mix of these forms of data?
5.	How will you analyse your data?
6.	Are participants aware of the time commitment and effort involved in completing the diary?
7.	Have you decided on content and structure and have you included this in your instructions?
8.	Are the instructions and terminology clear?
9.	Have you considered any specific requirements of the participant group you are targeting?
10.	Have you allowed time for developing and piloting your diary?

(Continued)

Table 2.1 Continued

11. How will you reinforce data recording and support participants throughout the data collection period (e.g. by regular personal or telephone contact)?

12. How will you address potential respondent fatigue?

13. How will you deal with attrition and partial completion of diaries?

14. Have you considered alternative formats to the written word?

Adapted from Nicholl (2010).

3 Practical issues with diary techniques: Design and analysis

Introduction

In previous chapters, we have discussed the different techniques that can be applied in using diary method for data collection. We have also discussed the methodological rationale for using the diary method. As illustrated, while solicited diaries are an established technique for gathering structured data on how often a particular activity or event occurs over a defined period of time, they can also provide important visual, semi- and unstructured and longitudinal insights. It is important, therefore, to think through some of the practical issues before planning to incorporate solicited diaries within your research design. When, for example, might solicited diary methods be appropriately used in designing your study? What approach should they take and what sorts of research questions they can be used to answer? How should participants return their diaries to you? How should you construct your diary and should solicited diaries be the sole method or part of a mixed methods study design? This latter point also raises important questions about the different ways in which solicited diaries might be analysed to maximize the insights that can be drawn from the data. Standard statistical, thematic and content analyses commonly used in quantitative and qualitative research can provide useful insights, but they also run the risk of losing the overarching narrative story and the longitudinal and temporal context that can be critical to understanding how and why events unfold over time. In addition, transcripts of audio diaries are typically much longer than written diaries, so the resources required to deal with this additional data need to be factored into the project design.

In this chapter, then, we consider some of the practicalities of using diary methods as part of your research design and provide guidance on analysing textual and visual data collected via this technique, including computer-assisted analysis. We draw on examples from recent research studies to consider not just traditional approaches to analysis, but how visual, time sequencing and narrative forms of analyses have been adopted to provide valuable and novel insights from this methodological technique.

Designing studies using diary techniques – what are the practicalities?

In what follows, we discuss some of the practical issues in designing and applying solicited diaries as a form of data collection. Firstly, it is important to consider the sorts of questions that solicited diary techniques can help to answer, whether as a single methodological technique or as part of a multi-method research design. Bolger et al. (2003) suggest a threefold typology of research questions that lend themselves to using solicited diary methods:

1. *Those designed to gain reliable individual information over time*

Using diary techniques can be useful where accuracy about an individual's experiences, practices, habits, actions and so forth are important to determine. Not only are solicited diaries less subject to the vagaries of memory, retrospective censorship or reframing of data given by participants than other methodological techniques, but they can also be useful where a researcher is interested in uncovering routine, everyday processes and events that may be viewed as trivial – and thus easily forgotten by the respondent (Milligan et al., 2005). In these circumstances, change over time may be less important than gaining an accurate and in-depth understanding of individual experiences of the phenomena of interest.

2. *Those designed to obtain an understanding of within-person change over time and individual differences in such change*

Here, solicited diaries can help to answer research questions where the focus is on gathering an accurate understanding of how a purposively defined range of individuals' thoughts, experiences, embodied actions and reactions, etc., to phenomena of interest may (or may not) change over time. Such individual-level data can then be used to analyse between-person differences in those experiences. Change over time and understanding between-person comparisons are at the core of this type of research question.

3. *Those designed to conduct causal analysis of within-person changes and individual differences in these changes*

Here, the focus is on understanding the underlying causes of changes within an individual in relation to the phenomena of interest and how these may vary between people. Time may play an important role in understanding an individual's embodied responses to internal factors (whether physical, cognitive or emotional) or external (social or environmental) factors. As Bolger et al. (2003) put it, 'diaries can help us to understand the antecedents, correlates and consequences of daily experiences' (p. 586). The emphasis of the research here, then, is to uncover the processes that underlie within-person variability.

Secondly, before adopting solicited diaries as part of any research design, it is important to think about the abilities of the research participants. As Jacelon and Imperio (2005) point out, written solicited diaries require, firstly, literacy – that is, the ability of participants to read and write in the language in which the study is being conducted. Secondly, they require physical capacity in terms of the vision to read and the hand co-ordination to record their diaries either on paper or electronically. This infers that diary techniques may be suitable only for more literate (and hence better-educated) participants, and, as such, can introduce a level of participant bias from the outset. However, claims that diary methods can be exclusionary are often overstated as researchers have demonstrated that with careful thought, this technique can be used successfully with so-called vulnerable groups, e.g. young disabled men (Gibson, 2002), children (Buchwald, 2009), people with dementia (Bartlett, 2012) and those with chronic fatigue syndrome (Kempke et al., 2013), to name but a few. This is an issue we return to in more detail in Chapter 5. Importantly, as we have already suggested, the solicited diary need not be confined to the written word where writing ability may act as a barrier to participation, rather audio and video diary alternatives can usefully be offered.

Taking a structured, semi-structured or unstructured approach to diary design

Having confirmed that solicited diaries will usefully and appropriately contribute to the overall goals of the study, you now need to think through which form/s or which diary technique are most appropriate for gathering the data required to achieve the research aims and objectives. Diaries may be highly structured – where all activities are pre-categorized by the research team – or they can be semi-structured and involve a mix of specific questions with an option for free text or they can be in an open format, enabling participants to record activities and events in their own words. A key question to be asked, then, is whether a structured, semi-structured or unstructured approach is most appropriate for your needs? For instance, are you interested in how many times specific events, phenomena or activities and their variables occur over a prescribed length of time? Or are you more interested in a person's thoughts, feelings or the unspoken and often personal actions or experiences that may not be deemed important by the respondent when engaging with more reactive research techniques? Is a visual record or recording of specific phenomena over time important to the research question? What part might new technologies play in your diary study? These sorts of questions will be important in helping you to decide whether a structured solicited diary in which predefined phenomena are recorded and counted over time is most appropriate to the gathering of the data you require, or whether a semi- or unstructured approach (either audio or written) to diary recording is more suitable. Additionally, you need to consider whether your study requires the gathering of more visual data over time – or indeed whether some combination of the above is required. How you structure your diary and the instructions given to your participants for the completion of their diaries will depend on the approach you take.

Structured approaches to diary keeping typically involve a lot of guidance and instructions for participants. Furthermore, individuals are expected to respond to predetermined questions and to keep their responses within the parameters of the study aims and topic. Below is an example of how a structured food diary may be designed in order to understand an individual's nutritional patterns over a prescribed period of time. As well as providing space for the information the participant is required to enter in a way that aids the quantification of data collection, the participant also needs to be given clear instructions on how he or she should complete it.

How to Complete Your Food Diary

➤ Please complete you food diary for X days in a row.
➤ Please avoid completing your diary over special times of the year that do not accurately reflect your regular eating patterns (such as birthdays, Xmas or other religious festivals or celebrations).
➤ Try to describe the food you eat and how it was prepared. For example, was it grilled, fried, boiled or roasted? If you had cereal did you add sugar and milk? What kind of bread, rice or pasta did you eat, e.g. brown, white? What kind of milk did you drink, e.g. skimmed, semi-skimmed, full fat? If you had a hot drink did you add milk and how many teaspoons of sugar?
➤ Your food diary should be a record of what you eat and drink each day and should include everything – even those things that you know are not as healthy for you as others.

Day & Date	Time	Food Description	Amount
Monday 16 September 2014	8.30 am	White toast butter and marmalade	2 pieces
		Boiled egg	1
		Coffee with milk and two sugars	1 cup
	10.30 am	Coffee with milk and two sugars	1 cup
		Muffin	1
	12.30 pm	Egg salad sandwich with butter and mayonnaise	2
		Crisps	1 small bag
		Orange juice	1 small carton
		Apple	1
	3.00 pm	Coffee with milk and two sugars	1 cup
		Chocolate biscuit	2
	5.30 pm	Lamb chops, roasted potatoes, carrots	Medium plate
		Green beans with gravy	Medium serving
		Apple pie with custard	
		Wine	1 glass
	8.30 pm	Cocoa	1 mug
		Plain digestive biscuit	2

However, while this kind of solicited diary can provide important informa-tion about the dietary habits of the individual over the course of a day and beyond, portion size and *perceptions* of portion size can differ. For instance, are the slices of bread taken at breakfast large or small? Are they thick or thin? Are the chocolate biscuits fully covered in chocolate or just top coated? Is the glass of wine a small glass or a large glass? This level of detail can be important where accuracy of actual intake is required. To address this issue, some researchers using structured diary techniques have incorporated visual data gathering (food photography) as part of their research design. Here, participants were asked to take photographs of their meals/snacks (often using disposable cameras) in order to gain a clearer picture of the size and detail of the actual food intake. Researchers may even provide extra equipment to ensure a consistent approach to food photography, such as a 12" ruler to be photographed next to the plate of food (Gregory, Walwyn, Bloor, & Amin, 2006) or a piece of premeasured string to standardize the distance from which photographs of food are taken (Small et al., 2009). In doing so, the visual data gathered from the food photography can be used to enhance the validity and reliability of the written diary data.

Qualitative approaches to the solicited diary also involve the participant being given a clear set of guidelines on how to complete the diary and the frequency with which this should be undertaken, but diary completion may take either a semi- or unstructured format depending on the purpose of the diary. Below is an example of a less structured approach involving adult carers. In less structured diaries, participants are given a set of head-ings or themes linked to the research objectives and asked to record their experiences of a phenomenon, their activities, thoughts, feelings and so on in relation to those themes at regular intervals over an agreed period of time. In many instances, participants are given the opportunity to include other issues that may not be part of the predefined themes, but which they feel are important to them in relation to the study aims.

Thank you for agreeing to help us with our study. We would like you to fill in your diary every evening for xxx consecutive days/weeks. If you are not able to fill in your diary on a particular evening, please try to fill it in as soon as possible the following day. If you miss several days, please do not give up, just start over again on the next day you are able to, and leave the pages for the missed days blank.

Here are some points we would like you to bear in mind when you are filling in your diary:

> We are interested in your day-to-day experiences of life while caring for your family member; this involves all of your daily experiences, not just those associated with your caregiving role.

> Remember that this is YOUR diary. We are interested in finding out as much as possible about the care and support you give to your loved one (physical and emotional), the support you receive on a daily basis from social and health-care services and your experiences of this support. This also includes your experiences of other forms of help or support that you may receive from the voluntary sector, friends, family and neighbours. We are also interested in how your caregiving role affects your own daily life, such as your ability to go out to work, to go out and socialize and your own health and well-being. So please tell us as much as you can about yourself – no matter how unimportant or repetitive it seems. For instance, if you have made plans to go shopping but then had to cancel it because the weather was too bad to take your loved one out and you had no one to sit with him or her, or if you felt under the weather and decided not to go, please tell us. We would rather have too much information than too little.

> We recognize that as a carer you may have little free time to yourself so please feel free to write as much or as little as you are able.

> Please don't worry about spelling, grammar or 'best' handwriting but try to write as clearly as you can, using a pen. Alternatively, if you prefer to write using a computer that is fine too.

> Please fill in the day and date in the space provided on each new diary page. NAME will arrange to collect your diary on a weekly basis.

If you have any questions about the diary, please phone NAME on TELEPHONE: XXXXX or email her at: EMAIL ADDRESS. She will return your call/contact so you do not have to pay for the call.

SEPARATE PAGE

Please enter the day and date here:

_____

Please write your daily diary entry here. (Please continue overleaf if necessary. You may write as much or as little as you are able.)

FREE TEXT

These two examples draw on opposite ends of the structured–unstructured diary continuum. Where appropriate, it is also possible to combine elements of both structured and unstructured data gathering in solicited diaries. Milligan et al. (2005) in their study of the impact of communal gardening and social activity on the well-being of older people, for example, sought to gather unstructured weekly diary data on people's engagement with a social and a communal gardening activity intervention. However, they were also keen to assess the potential impact on participants' health and well-being over time. To facilitate this, the diary was designed to ask participants to complete a short series of structured questions from a validated health and well-being survey at the beginning of each weekly diary entry. This was followed by a series of semi-structured themes designed to encourage participants to write about their experiences and feelings related to their engagement with the gardening activity and other activities they had been involved in over the course of that week.

Unstructured approaches to diary keeping take a similar approach but with the participant simply being asked to record at regular defined intervals whatever he or she feels is important/relevant in relation to the phenomena of interest without additional prompts. Thomas (2007) took an unstructured approach in her investigation into living with HIV-related illnesses in Namibia. Participants were informed of the broad aims of the study, but the researcher made it clear that they could write whatever they liked in their diaries (p. 77). A key advantage of the unstructured, free format diary approach is that it allows for greater opportunity to recode and analyse the data. However, the labour-intensive work required to prepare and make sense of the data may make it an unrealistic option for research projects where time and resources are limited, or where the study sample is large (Corti, 1993).

Issues of completion and submission of diary data

Whatever the design or structure of the solicited diary, careful thought needs to be given to the frequency and time span over which diary completion should take place. Requesting participants to complete detailed data too often over too long a period of time can result in poor or non-completion and dropout. Conversely, leaving too long a gap between diary completion not only can result in dropout, but can also be subject to the problems of recall failure. Giving careful consideration to: (a) the time span an event or activity can be accurately recalled by a participant; (b) the length of time a research project needs to gather data in order to meet its objectives (e.g. Are different times of the day, week, month or year important?); and (c) the length of time a participant can reasonably be asked to continue completing diaries is therefore critical to the success of the solicited diary method. Yet these are not always easy questions to answer, and while some researchers maintain the dangers of respondent fatigue means that diaries are only successful when completed over relatively short periods of time, such as one or two weeks (e.g. Keleher & Verrinder, 2003), others have demonstrated that with the right rationale, incentive and support, diary data can be successfully gathered over an extended period of time. For instance, in a study of:

- professional identity formation amongst medical students, weekly audio diaries were successfully gathered from 17 medical students over a period of **18 months** (Monrouxe, 2009);
- the 2001 foot and mouth epidemic in the UK, weekly diaries were successfully gathered from 54 participants drawn from farming and related rural communities affected by the disaster, also over an **18-month period** (Mort, Convery, Baxter, & Bailey, 2005);
- household consumption and expenditure in Gambia and Tanzania, some participants chose to keep a diary for **12 months** because they were keen to show the researcher the effects of seasonality on their economic well-being (Wiseman et al., 2005);
- crying and mood, 97 female participants kept a crying and mood diary that ranged from **40 to 73 days**, corresponding to the duration of two consecutive menstrual cycles (Bylsma, Croon, Vingerhoets, & Rottenberg, 2011);
- sport stressors and coping strategies, 13 female adolescent athletes maintained a weekly audio diary for **one season – 16 weeks** (Tamminen & Holt, 2010);
- gardening and social activity amongst older people, as referred to earlier, weekly diaries were gathered from around 100 participants over a **nine-month period** (Milligan et al., 2005).

So, there is no 'right' or 'wrong' period of time for keeping a diary. Each study will be different, and you will need to decide for yourself the methodological rationale and resources that will be required for whatever time frame you decide upon.

Critically, in each of the studies listed, it made methodological sense for people to maintain a diary for an extended period of time; participants were not being asked to keep a diary over a relatively long time just for the sake of it. In the study of crying and mood, for example, the goal was to repeatedly sample crying episodes from everyday life. This was achieved as within the 1,007 diary entries generated, every participant cried at least once, and for many individuals multiple crying episodes were reported (Bylsma et al., 2011, p. 391). These episodes may not have been captured if participants had been asked to keep their diary for only one or two weeks. Likewise, it made methodological sense to collect data over the course of an entire season when investigating stressors and coping strategies amongst athletes (Tamminen & Holt, 2010). Hence, the duration of data collection is an important methodological consideration in diary design.

Moreover, in each of the studies listed, a member of the research team regularly engaged with participants to advise on progress, check up on a participant where a diary had not been submitted (e.g. due to illness or holidays) and to encourage continuation of diary submission throughout the life-course of the project. Additionally, in the study by Mort et al. (2005), they were also able to provide a small sum of money for each weekly diary completed in acknowledgement of the work involved in completing the diaries. This was paid to participants on monthly visits to gather the diaries. We return to this topic of providing financial incentives to participants in Chapter 5. The point here is that with appropriate support measures in place, concerns about respondent fatigue can be addressed enabling solicited diaries to be used as a research tool over fairly long periods of time.

Diary completion and submission has, in the past, tended to be in the form of a handwritten, paper-based diary that is either collected at agreed intervals by a member of the research team or posted to the research team in prepaid envelopes. Advances in technology and people's familiarity with, and access to, the internet, email and other modern means of communication has meant that while some participants may still prefer to handwrite their submissions, there has been an increased adoption of diary completion and submission in electronic formats. This has the advantage of increasing the turnaround time of submission, reducing the need for transcription of the written diary and for increasing communication options through email and so forth. Even where video and audio diaries are undertaken in personal settings, the use of the electronic submission is increasing. However, these developments also raise issues of data security that is of increasing concern to ethical review boards and hence cannot be ignored. We return to this in Chapter 4.

Where audio- or video-diary techniques are adopted, the research team needs to ensure that diarists have access to portable and easy-to-use voice or video recording equipment. This may take the form of equipment delivered to each participant and collected by the research team over the agreed period of time for diary completion (e.g. Williamson, Leeming, Lyttle, & Johnson, 2012); by giving participants an individual (video) tape that can be used with a smaller number of shared video or audio equipment in an agreed setting (e.g. Roberts, 2011); or by setting up a single set of equipment in a space that is accessible to all participants (e.g. a workplace or social setting) and which can be used at a time suitable by all participants (Brennan et al., 2010). As discussed in Chapter 4, the emergence in recent years of low cost or freely available computer software apps that can either video or audio record data also opens up wider opportunities for the use of these options given the increasing number of households with access to computers and the internet.

Finally, when designing a diary-based study, it is important not to overlook the important but practical matter of how you will get completed diaries back. This can be a real challenge for researchers, as participants will need clear instructions as to how they should return their diary and any diary-keeping equipment to you. Moreover, even if clear return instructions are supplied, there is no guarantee that participants will return their diaries and equipment without additional reminders or some encouragement. One researcher highlighted the challenges of getting back tape recorders and audio diaries from a group of twenty-four participants with visual impairment; she noted that 'while many were returned promptly, just as many took upwards of months to come back as participants contacted the researcher to say they were "busy with work and school"' (Worth, 2009). In this case, all but one of the audio diaries were eventually returned. However, it does illustrate some of the challenges that can arise in getting both data and equipment back and how important it is to plan ahead and factor in time for participants to return their diaries to you.

Dealing with variation and missing data in diary completion

It is worth noting that people approach diary keeping in very different ways. Those adopting semi- or unstructured diary methods will find that there can be considerable variation in the length of entry and the degree of personal revelations a person will enter into the diary. For example, some diarists may take a very reflective approach to their diary keeping that conveys their feelings and emotions around their experiences of the phenomena of interest, while others will write shorter, more straightforward and factual account of events (Milligan et al., 2005). This difference in approach to diary entry is perhaps reflective of two things: firstly, as Sheridan (1993) noted several decades ago, some people will inevitably be more predisposed to being diarists than others and will use the opportunity to reflect on their everyday lives, while others may view it as a more boring and repetitive activity to be undertaken as quickly as possible. Secondly, the length of time diarists are able or willing to devote to completion may depend on what else is going on in their lives versus the time they can devote to what needs to be a regular task over a specific time period.

The latter point also raises the important issue of non-completion and how this is dealt with in the analysis. In structured approaches, it is important that non-completion is recorded prior to analysis in the same way you would approach non-completion in other forms of statistical data analysis. In more qualitative approaches, it is important to consider the extent to which this non-completion impacts on the overall temporal flow of the diary. In a longitudinal study. if there is a simply one week of missing data, it may be possible to discover why this occurred (e.g. due to illness or holiday). While it is important to acknowledge these missing data, it may have limited impact on the overall diary keeping. If, however, the diary was completed over a fairly short timescale, for example days or a few weeks, then large chunks of missing data may significantly affect the veracity of the temporal narrative in which case the diary in question may need to be discarded. Where missing data falls somewhere between these two extremes, there will inevitably be a judgement call to be made. In these instances, it is important to consider how reliable the remaining data is in terms of its contribution to the wider study. On such occasions, peer scrutiny of the data with other members of your research team (if relevant) or a research colleague may be a useful way of confirming whether or not the data are sufficiently reliable to include.

Analysing diary data

Techniques and the resources required to analyse diary data will depend on the approach taken, the purpose for which the diary has been constructed and the size of the research team. In projects where one sole researcher is analysing written diary data on his or her own the process is relatively straightforward. However, projects involving multiple team members and forms of data are likely to be complex and require greater practical effort so materials can be shared (Pink, 2009). For example, for many large-scale structured diaries, following diary submission there is an intensive process of editing which includes checking entries against the structured questions and entering onto a database. Where a structured diary has been adopted with the objective of counting actions, events and so forth, the diary data can be either descriptively analysed or more commonly analysed using statistical (often regression) techniques. A study by Tennen, Affleck, Coyne, Larsen, and Delongis (2006) of depression history and daily reactions to pain amongst women with fibromyalgia, for example, used structured daily diaries with scaled responses to a series of preset questions over a thirty-day period. The data were then analysed using multilevel analyses to address within-person relations; these data were then scaled up to give generalized results. As Wickham and Knee (2013) point out, even where you may be using structured approaches, one of the strengths of solicited diary method is the temporal nature of the data gathered and recognizing that the data are realized both 'in the moment' and over time. They highlight how important it is to recognize this in the analysis and argue that examining temporal processes in the diary data enables a much more nuanced understanding of events or processes. For instance, it is possible to examine lagged effects that facilitate more dynamic research questions such as 'Does yesterday's experience/action etc. influence today's?' (p. 1184). This allows for a deeper analysis of within-person variance.

While statistical approaches to analysis are more commonly applied to structured diaries, they can also be applied as one element of the analyses of more semi- or unstructured diaries. Here, it may be important not just to understand how events or phenomena unfold in the diarist's own words, but also, for example, to consider how many times he or she refers to the specific phenomenon of interest. Linguists may also be concerned not just with the unfolding story, but also with an analysis of the language used and the frequency of particular elements of that language. However, it is also possible to use these more linguistic approaches to diary analysis in other ways, such as discourse analysis. This may be particularly appropriate where the research design makes use of audio diaries where *how* an entry is recorded, the tone of speech used in recording the diary entry etc. may be as important as what is said.

Within semi- and unstructured approaches to solicited diaries, the objective is to analyse the more free flowing data, whether written (electronically or on paper) or oral. Following transcription, this can be undertaken through either traditional thematic or constant comparative approaches, where the core technique is to examine, compare and cat-egorize data until no new categories emerge. The overall aim is to identify themes arising either within an individual's data over time or across a sam-ple of participants with similar or differing characteristics. This involves the coding of verbatim entries. Processing can be very labour-intensive, in much the same way as it is for processing semi-structured or unstruc-tured interview transcripts. Using highly trained coders and a rigorous unambiguous coding scheme is very important, particularly where there is no clear demarcation of events or behaviour in the diary entries. Where appropriate, a well-designed diary with a coherent pre-coding system can help to reduce the degree of editing and coding required.

However, it is important to bear in mind that while thematic and constant comparative approaches to analysis are useful for identifying themes in the data set, this type of approach relies on cutting up data by code or thematically to achieve an across-person analysis. While this can be a useful and valid approach, as with other narrative approaches, it can also result in the loss of the personal story and temporality of that story that is being told through the diary. As a consequence some researchers choose to adopt a narrative approach to the analysis, where the researcher attempts to make sense of the storylines or narrative threads that run longitudinally through the diary in order to convey the meaning and contextual detail that is important to understanding and explaining the storylines that run through the diary (Thomas, 2007).

Factors to consider when analysing video, photo and audio diaries

Video, photo and audio diaries require a slightly different approach to analysis. Video diaries produce moving images as well as spoken words that need to be sifted through and coded. While photo diaries obviously produce still images which are meaningful to the participant, they also require sifting through and coding in some way. Audio diaries produce significant amounts of monologue and often contain background sounds, which may or may not be important to decipher. Thus, the basic approach to analysing audiovisual materials is the same as that required for the analysis of data collected through conventional methods – that is, 'a process of abstraction' in which the audio diary will need to be transcribed, and the research team will need to select and follow some kind of systematic coding process (Pink, 2009, p. 120). The main difference, however, is that there is an 'increased complexity in the data' collected from audiovisual materials, and so the task is likely to be more time-consuming and requires the researcher to do more filtering of what is not required for the study (Noyes, 2004, p. 203). Moreover, audiovisual materials are 'evocative' and thus one's whole body and sensory range is likely to be engaged in the interpretative process (see Pink, 2009 for a more detailed discussion). In fact, one of the first issues to consider in the analysis of audiovisual materials is your reaction as a researcher to what you see and hear in the diary. The process of identifying and noting the parts of a diary that you find most compelling, and why, adds another important layer of meaning-making. As one researcher explains,

> I endeavoured to gain an initial sense of common themes across photo diaries, noting images that seemed incongruous or different. I also documented images that drew my attention. Reflecting on why such images interested me in conjunction with participants' explanations provided insights into young people's critique of some factors of school's sexual culture. (Allen, 2009, p. 490/1).

As well as reflecting on what fascinates you about the data, it is important to note any negative reactions too. This is what a team of researchers had to do in their photo-interview-diary study of child labour in the UK. As they reported, 'A first viewing of the selected images produced in us, the researchers, a sense of disappointment. Images of the children working were scarce; indeed shots containing people of any kind were a minority' (Mizen, 2005, p. 128). They had expected – or perhaps hoped – to see more images of the children actually working, as this is what the children had spoken of in their interviews. However, on reflection, they soon realized that the children's photographs provided 'visual substance and tangible detail to what, for researchers at least, has tended to be as much instinctively as substantively known: i.e. the environments and to some extent the character of children's work' (p. 129). Thus, the visual data opened another way of knowing, one based on what the participant actually saw while they were working, rather than what the researcher imagined they could see.

Where diary studies combine diary method with other methods of data collection, such as interviews and participant observation, a deeper understanding can be achieved during the process of data analysis, as the researcher will vacillate between, and simultaneously explore, both the visual and textual diary and non-diary data in order to make sense of the topic. This is evident not only in the quotes we have included above, but also in other studies that have combined visual diary method with interviews, such as those we refer to below. In these examples, we show how diaries provide scope to look at, and analyse, the interaction between image and text (Plowman & Stevenson, 2012).

> Combinations of visual, audio and written data permit multilevel analysis, allowing the researcher literally and metaphorically to 'zoom in' on individual children's uses of different communicative modes with different people, at particular activities in particular moments of time, to 'pan out' by observing the children over time and across different social settings and to explore the relations between these different perspectives (Flewitt, 2006, p. 29).

> When filming was completed I worked with the video diary footage in two ways. As research data, each of the video diaries was transcribed, integrated with interview and journal data and analysed thematically. By identifying categories and concepts across the different methods I was able to support my interpretation of the video diaries with other data and consider them within a broader context (Bates, 2013, p. 34).

A second factor to consider in the analysis of audiovisual materials is the subject matter – that is, scrutinizing what is actually visible and audible within an image or film. Such an approach constitutes a basic content analysis and many researchers use the technique to assess the frequency of particular people, places or objects (Plowman & Stevenson, 2012). Aldridge (2007) used the technique in her analysis of 471 images taken by adults with learning disabilities using disposable cameras for a study of a gardening service. By conducting a basic content analysis, the researcher identified various categories and subcategories, such as indoor and outdoor gardening activity, tools and transport, all of which described the subject matter of the images; 42 per cent of the images contained people, and so one conclusion drawn was of the significance of 'social activity' for adults with learning disabilities (p. 9). A sophisticated and well-established example of content analysis is Video Intervention/Prevention Assessment (VIA) described below. Content analysis is a useful and popular technique, then, for making sense of audiovisual materials.

Video Intervention/Prevention Assessment (VIA) is a qualitative research method that investigates health conditions from the patient's perspective. VIA's primary data consist of visual illness narratives, video diaries made by participants of their experiences living with and managing chronic medical conditions. The visual narratives are viewed and listened to by a data logger and notated in sequential scenes by participant identification number, tape number, and video time code. The content of the audio visual data is logged as text comprising 'objective descriptions' of information that is visible or audible and 'subjective accounts' of what is observed, relating the participant's perspective, emotional tone and psychosocial dynamics of a scene. Within the logs, distinct font headings designate different types of data, so that they can be recognized as such when the logs are imported into NVivo qualitative analysis software for data management, structuring and analysis. Using this software, multiple researchers can code, recode and refine the logs of the visual illness narratives and link their structured analyses to illustrative excerpts from the primary audiovisual data (Rich & Patashnick, 2002, p. 245).

As well as paying attention to content, it is important to bear in mind the action required on the part of the participant to produce audiovisual diary materials and how this might affect the quality of data. Several researchers comment on the dynamic or performative elements of producing a video diary or posing for an image as part of your diary recording – and the importance of taking this account when analysing your data. For example, in one video-diary study involving primary school children, the researcher noticed how the young participants had a tendency to perform in front of the camera, particularly in the earlier stages of data collection while they were still getting used to the novelty (Noyes, 2004). Other researchers who have used video-diary method have found that adult participants (particularly men) may be self-conscious about filming themselves (Roberts, 2011). While this is not a problem in itself, it may be important for you to consider when making decisions about the duration of diary keeping, in order that you allow time for participants to get used to the diary-keeping process. So, when it comes to analysis there will be sufficient naturalistic data to interpret.

Given the complexity and variety of data produced by video and photo diaries, some researchers will purposively select certain aspects of the data to analyse, as opposed to trying to make sense of every single aspect of the data set. With this approach, rather than embracing the complexity of visual data, researchers endeavour to simplify the process. Roberts (2011), for example, approached the analysis of visual diary data collected from university students by focusing on what students *said* in their videos (our emphasis), and made no attempt to analyse anything but the more 'obvious visual components of the diary such as who was present and whether someone was laughing or crying' (p. 681). Similarly, the research team who used video-diary method to investigate young girls' experiences of running away from home focused on what the girls spoke about, rather than trying to make sense of the performative elements of the diaries (Edinburgh et al., 2013). In the main, then, this approach focuses on transcribing and analysing the spoken word in much the same way as an audio diary is analysed, picking up on only the most obvious of visual cues. The key rationale for using visual diaries in such cases may thus be less about the importance or relevance of visual analysis and more about the appropriateness of this type of diary tech-nique for the particular group or individuals being studied. However, it is also common for researchers who have used photo-diary method to sift through images with the participant himself or herself and select a sam-ple for a more detailed depth analysis (photo elicitation). We would sug-gest that novice researchers, especially those conducting the research on their own, take a more simplified approach to the analysis of audiovisual materials to make the process manageable, moving on to more complex forms of analysis once they feel comfortable with the process or are doing so as part of a larger team of experienced researchers.

Finally, it is important to consider data management, especially the stor-age of data and sharing of files.[1] Audiovisual diaries typically create very large files which will need to be kept securely on PCs with a firewall system and password-encrypted data files. You therefore need to feel confident about having the equipment and skills to do this when designing and resourcing your project, enlisting the help and advice of a data technician if necessary. It is also worth emphasizing that researchers typically have audio and video diaries transcribed verbatim, so there will be a text file (as well as audio and video file) per diary. All of this highlights the importance of deciding how and where you will store data safely and systematically at the outset of the study.

In terms of actually managing and sifting the data collected through visual and photo diaries, depending on the size and nature of the study, researchers who work with audiovisual materials typically either develop some kind of matrix on a spreadsheet or in a Word file or use computer-assisted software programs like NVivo or Atlas to facilitate data analysis. Regardless of whether a structured, semi-structured or unstructured approach is taken, the aim is always the same: to use and conduct a systematic analysis of multiple data sources to develop an understanding of the phenomenon under investigation (Alaszewski, 2006b). Below are a few selected examples of how researchers who have collected audio (visual) materials using diary method have approached the management, storage and coding of data.

In a structured study of well-being amongst Chinese students using an online diary, participants were asked to identity and rate the range of emotions they had experienced during the course of a week, data were analysed using the specialist computerized program – Linguistic Inquiry and Word Count – which can 'handle large volumes of open-ended responses at greatly reduced speeds, without sacrificing consistency in coding' (Tov, Ng, Lin, & Qiu, 2013, p. 1069).

In a semi-structured study of the transition from medical student to junior doctor using a combination of interviews and audio diaries:

> A thematic index was developed to which the entire dataset could be coded. Twenty-five initial categories were devised by the research team and the eight individual researchers subsequently developed thematic indices according to their own understanding of the emerging content of the data. A final overall indexing system was discussed and agreed by all parties in a collaborative research

meeting prior to the first stage of formal analysis. Data were then coded to the individual categories in the thematic framework using NVivo, a computerised indexing system for qualitative data (Brennan et al., 2010, p. 453).

In an unstructured study of visually impaired young people's transition to adulthood using audio diaries, diaries were analysed alongside other data sources as part of a participant case, using an experience-centred approach to thematic narrative analysis (Worth, 2009).

Further discussion of data analysis is beyond the scope of this book. However, techniques for making sense of diaries as a data source and the issues raised by the development and use of specialist computerized programs will be of increasing importance as diary methods diversify and researchers embrace digital forms of data collection. In the next chapter, we discuss the rise of technology and its impact on diary method and make further reference to the process of data analysis in the context of digital technologies.

4 The rise of technology and its influences on diary methods

Introduction

In this chapter, we consider how the influences of technology and social media are changing the nature of diary keeping and impacting on diary-based research. Drawing on the growing body of literature concerned with electronic diaries, capture technologies (such as cameras and mobile phones), internet-based research and web-based applications, we discuss how emerging technologies and modern forms of communication, including microblogging, all have the potential to change the meaning and nature of diary keeping and the potential medium through which diary data might be gathered. As we increasingly record our actions, feelings and experiences – both visually and in written format – on the internet, our inner thoughts and private lives become increasingly more public and immediately accessible, leaving them open to scrutiny and interpretation by others. The introduction of the Facebook timeline provides just one example of how people's lives are being chronologically constructed and recorded through the internet. The proliferation of 'selfies' on Instagram and other photo sharing sites is another new development in human behaviour, which has a potential bearing on diary method. However, these technologies also bring with them ethical and reliability challenges that cannot be overlooked. In this chapter, then, we begin by discussing why and how technologies are used in diary-based research before considering these issues and how these technologies are opening up a new medium through which diary methods might be applied and data gathered.

Technological trends in diary-based research

In the last decade, the application of technologies in diary-based studies has expanded enormously. Since 2000, there has been a significant rise in published diary studies involving technologies, with the majority of studies published since 2007. Reviewing this literature, the application of technologies in diary-based research can be divided into three broad trends. The first of these is computerized or electronic diaries using hand-held devices, such as the Palm. Handheld devices first came out in 1996 and researchers began using them soon afterwards. The second trend is that of 'capture' technology such as cameras, voice recorders and mobile (smart) phones; these technologies are developing at an extremely rapid pace, but diary-based researchers saw their potential some time ago (Brown, Sellen, & O'hara, 2000). The third trend involves online and web-based technologies. A closer examination of each of these applications will help to elucidate how these technologies are changing the nature of diary keeping and impacting on diary-based research.

Computerized or electronic diaries using handheld devices

One of the most well-established technological trends in diary-based research is computerized or electronic diaries using a handheld device. There are several types of handheld device available, but they have in common time-set features and allow items (such as questions and auditory alarms) to be programmed in. Users enter data using a touchscreen and stylus. The latest models are equipped with Wi-Fi and GPS capabilities and other advanced functions and features. The widespread use of this technology is evidenced by the fact that specific software packages have been developed for researchers, as described below. Thus, electronic handheld devices or computers provide researchers with a potentially ideal way of capturing quality diary data in a rigorous and systematic way.

> With the proliferation of PDA devices, there are PDA software programmes that have been developed specifically to conduct diary studies. One software package that is readily available, and regarded as particularly useful for marital and family research, is the Experience Sampling Programme (ESP). ESP is a free and user-friendly programme for running basic diary studies on PDAs with little or no software programme experience (Laurenceau & Bolger, 2005, p. 93).

Computerized or electronic diaries are often used in structured diary studies to capture numerical data and assess variables. In such studies, the diary functions as a survey: participants respond to predetermined questions set by the researcher. For instance, in one study of the link between alcohol use and intimate partner violence, participants were asked to complete a structured diary over a sixty-day period about their alcohol and drug use on a daily basis using a Palm Z22 handheld computer. Participants were trained to use the device and each participant designated a time to be prompted by an alarm to complete the diary (when privacy was ensured and compliance would be maximized) (Moore, Elkins, McNulty, Kivisto, & Handsel, 2011). A total of 8,280 diary entries were received and the researchers found that the 'improved power that comes with assessing variables on a daily basis' improved the quality of data (p. 325). Researchers tend to use electronic diaries to answer research questions that are too complex to answer by simpler designs but are sufficiently simple to gain meaningful answers from the data it is possible to collect (Burton, Weller, & Sharpe, 2007, p. 559).

There is a vast body of literature pertaining to the use of electronic diaries in health and social research. This suggests that electronic diaries hold the potential to gain more accurate data than interviews alone about the associations between variables, such as the process of symptom experience (Burton et al., 2007). Take, for instance, a study of stress and triggers in children with headache disorders, in which handheld computers were programmed to signal an auditory alarm three times per day (just after awakening, after school/afternoon and before bedtime) at individually tailored times that were established with the child during the initial study visit. Times could be set differently for weekdays and weekends if requested by the child (Connelly & Bickel, 2011, p. 856). By using an electronic (as opposed to paper) diary, the researchers were able to programme questions about sleep in the morning assessment and test assumptions generated by other studies about the associations between triggers and symptoms.

Other areas of the literature discuss electronic versus paper-based diaries and the advantages of one over the other. The general consensus is that electronic diaries are not necessarily 'better' than paper-based diaries but they can be more useful (than paper diaries) in certain study designs. This includes studies that 'place a high premium on equally spaced reports', as an electronic diary allows the researcher to verify the time of completion (Green, Rafaeli, Bolger, Shrout, & Reis, 2006, p. 104) – the study of stress and triggers in children with headache disorders would fall into this category – and studies that require participants to remember to make several entries over the course of one day. For example, in one study of female patients with an eating disorder, participants were asked to complete a brief questionnaire about their emotional state and urged to be physically active nine times a day when signalled to do so by the electronic device they were given (Vansteelandt, Rijmen, Pieters, Probst, & Vanderlinden, 2007). The stratified time sampling procedure, and in particular, the frequency of reporting allowed the research team to identify some key characteristics about living with an eating disorder (p. 1721). Moreover, because data had been collected electronically, the research team were able to verify the time of entries, minimize the time between an experience and the recording of it and thus have more confidence in the validity of the data set than would have been possible if sourced from paper diaries.

Electronic devices are used, then, because they can the enhance quality of data. They do this not only by producing verifiable data entries but also by increasing compliance. Generally speaking, researchers find that after a short amount of training (approximately twenty minutes) most participants can use electronic devices with ease, making retention more likely. The training procedure is likely to involve demonstration of the device and a chance to practice using it, as these researchers did:

> During the training session, each participant was asked to practice responding on a training Palm Pilot, on which a sample diary was installed. This was done to illustrate that the responses, once entered, were irretrievable, both by the participant and by his or her partner. During the practice sessions, the experimenter reviewed the entire diary, item by item, explaining each style of question and allowing participants to ask any questions about word or item meanings. Participants were encouraged to repeat the diary as many times as they needed until they felt comfortable with the device and with the meanings of the items. (Howland & Rafaeli, 2010, p. 1446)

Compliance in this study of empathy between couples was high; of a total of 21 possible days, couples fully responded on average 18.5 days (Howland & Rafaeli, 2010). Similarly, in another electronic diary study, in which researchers developed three web-based interventions aimed at increasing patient's self-management skills and quality of life, researchers found a high adherence to the diary protocol (83 per cent) particularly with older people and shorter diaries (Nes, Eide, Kristjánsdóttir, & van Dulmen, 2013). Compliance is critical for a diary-based study; it means the data set is more complete: there is less missing data, which is vital when it comes to the analysis of data as valid conclusions can be drawn about the phenomenon under investigation.

In terms of data analysis, because the study design is typically structured and aimed at capturing numerical data, statistical techniques and packages tend to be used to make sense of data sourced from electronic diaries. Indeed, one advantage of using an electronic diary is that diary data can go directly to a database, such as SPSS, thereby reducing the cost of data coding (Rönkä et al., 2010). Once diary entries have been transferred, cleaned and checked for completeness, researchers can begin the process of analysis, which typically involves examining for associations. Take, for instance, a study of spousal support amongst patients with Type 2 diabetes. Using descriptive analyses, researchers calculated the number of spouses who reported providing diet-related support, persuasion and pressure during the 24-day electronic diary period, before using multilevel modelling to test study hypotheses related to the links between spousal support and diabetic-related distress (Stephens et al., 2013). In this way, the electronic diary can speed up and enhance the analytical process by reducing the amount of time required to prepare the data set.

Although electronic devices can yield reliable data, it would be wrong to conclude that the quality of data gained from using a computerized diary is inevitably better. A study into the effectiveness of paper and electronic diary modes suggests that rather than making the blanket assumption that paper diaries are untrustworthy or old-fashioned, researchers should take a more 'moderate position' and select the diary mode that 'best suits the needs of the participant and researcher' (Green et al., 2006, p. 102). Other researchers agree and suggest more work is needed to resolve the methodological issues around paper and pencil versus electronic diaries (Laurenceau & Bolger, 2005). This view is helpful, as it takes account of the demands that computerized diary keeping can place on participants, and recognizes the continued utility of pen-and-paper diary method in the digital age.

With the emergence of technology in diary studies, it is also important to bear in mind that there is risk of alienating certain populations who may not use, or feel uncomfortable using, electronic devices on a regular basis. This might include, for example, frail older people, populations with lower levels of income, educational attainment and higher levels of mistrust, those whose religious or cultural beliefs mitigate against the use of electronic equipment at certain times (such as members of the Jewish community) and others who may feel uncomfortable about having to use an electronic device at certain times of the day (before going to bed, for example). Thus, technologies can adversely affect the nature of the relationship between the researcher and researched, if they are used unthinkingly, insensitively or without providing adequate training and support.

It has been suggested that if the population you are studying is not used to electronic devices, then paper-based diaries may generate better quality data (Green et al., 2006). Correspondingly, if the population you are involving are comfortable with technologies then it might be better to avoid using paper-based methods. That said, researchers should avoid stereotyping or assuming that certain populations (such as older people) are unable to use technology. Instead, it may be worthwhile piloting your research questions and methods of data collection with your target population, in order to ascertain which is most likely to be the best diary method to use.

Use of capture technologies such as cameras, voice recorders and mobile (smart) phones

Advances in technology mean there are increasingly more devices available that allow for the capture of a wide range of information and media; these include analogue and digital cameras, mobile phones and smartphones and voice recorders, collectively referred to here on in as 'capture technologies' (Brown et al., 2000). At the same time, and as noted in Chapter 2, there is a growing interest in sensory methodologies. Together these trends mean that increasing numbers of researchers are using capture technologies in diary-based research as a means of eliciting information and enabling participation.

One of the most well-established applications of capture technology in diary-based research is the video-diary method. Essentially this involves participants keeping a diary of an activity or experience using a video camera for an agreed period of time. Researchers have used video diary to explore the bodily experiences of running (Bates, 2013) and children's experiences of various life events (Buchwald, 2009), such as running away from home (Edinburgh et al., 2013) and learning in school (Noyes, 2004).

The video-diary method privileges action and the visible and is therefore an 'ideal device, with which to unlock bodily experience and bring the sensuous and affective qualities of embodiment to the screen' (Bates, 2013, p. 31). Video diary is a unique and innovative mode of data collection. It is fundamentally different from a paper-based diary, in that it generates moving data and allows for the visualization of phenomena. As such, video-capture technology is contributing to the diversification of diary-based research.

Another common application of capture technology in diary-based research is the photo diary. This involves participants taking photographs, which capture their experiences and activities, and usually talking to the researcher about them afterwards – a technique known as photo elicitation (Prosser & Schwartz, 1998). The approach originated in anthropology and ethnography and is popular with visual researchers. The following studies are just a few examples of how photo diaries are used to investigate areas of academic interest:

- twenty-two secondary school children in New Zealand were issued with disposable cameras to explore sexualities and school culture (Allen, 2009);
- twenty-two parents of preschool-aged children were asked to keep a photographic diary to record their child's dietary intake (Small et al., 2009); and
- three households in Sweden kept a photo diary of their family bulletin boards to research this form of communication (Nässla & Carr, 2003).

With photo-diary method, some researchers will use analogue (disposable) cameras, while others prefer to use digital cameras. The latter is probably the better of the two options as society becomes more and more digitalized. However, both options may rely on the researcher having access to sufficient numbers of cameras to disperse to all participants and therefore can have cost implications (see Table 4.1 for an overview of the strengths and limitations of each method).

Another relatively new development in diary-based research is the use of mobile phone technology. Several studies have used mobile phones to generate data about activities of research interest; in each case, participants were prompted to send information at specified intervals using a mobile phone. For example, Plowman and Stevenson (2012) recruited fourteen households with children aged three to four years to their

Toys and Technology study; the researchers sent text prompts six times at varying intervals between nine and five on the prearranged day and asked participants to respond within thirty minutes with a picture of their child along with text (p. 543). Similarly, a group of Finnish researchers recruited twenty-seven families with adolescent children to their mobile diary programme about family dynamics. It involved participants answering a series of questions via short text messages over the course of one week. Other researchers have used mobile phone technology to capture information about children's pain; twenty-two children aged eight years and over who had recurrent pain for at least three months received a text message six times a day for a week instructing them to report their pain in numeric values (Alfvén, 2010). It is noteworthy that in these studies, there were no, or very few, dropouts which suggests that mobile phone technology is an effective data collection tool, especially with children and young people. Moreover, in all these studies participants used their own mobile phone which helped to reduce costs and the need for training.

Finally, it is worth mentioning that there has been some use of voice-mail functionality in diary-based research. In the voice-mail method, participants use mobile or landline phones to make reports to a dedicated voice-mail line instead of recording events on paper (Palen, Salzman, & Street, 2002). In this article by Palen et al., researchers report using the method in two separate studies: the *Going Wireless Study*, which investigated novice users' experience of adapting to mobile telephony over a six-week period, and the *Wireless Life-Cycle Panel Study*, which was an extension of the original study, involving 200 novice users of mobile telephony (pp. 89/90). The method was used alongside semi-structured interviews and generated useful data about people's use of mobile phones. However, we could find no other studies that have used this approach, which suggests it is an unusual, possibly outdated or ineffective, mode of data collection in diary-based research.

Web-based platforms and applications

Another growing trend is internet-based diary research and the use of emails, web-based applications and social sharing sites such as Facebook and blogs to generate data. Diary researchers recognize that such applications are useful platforms for not only gathering valuable data but also recruiting participants. Participants to an internet-based migraine headache study (described below) were recruited, for example, via online discussion boards and websites; indeed, the whole process, including consenting participants to the study, collecting data and diaries, was conducted electronically. Such studies show how internet-based diary research allows the researcher to explore people's lives and 'access the social at a distance' (Bancroft, Karels, Meadhbh, & Jade, 2014, p. 139). This kept costs down and reduced the potential demands of face-to-face communication on the participant.

> A conventional headache diary was formatted for the internet to collect daily headache data over four months using a time-series design. Women between eighteen and fifty-five years who were not pregnant or post-menopausal, and whose headaches met migraine criteria, were recruited primarily via the Internet, completed online consent forms, and were screened via telephone. They completed health history questionnaires and daily diary pages containing scales and open-ended questions, which were saved to a database (Moloney et al., 2009, p. 693).

Other researchers have used email function to collect diarized data, which again removes the practicalities and costs associated with collecting a physical diary. Such studies are carried out in a similar way to a paper-based diary but rely entirely on email communication. Take, for instance, a relatively unstructured study of aftercare received by patients who underwent inpatient psychotherapy treatment; the 297 participants recruited to the study were instructed thus: 'Once a week on your fixed writing day, please take 15 to 30 minutes to write an e-mail to your therapist. Write about your deepest thoughts and feelings about the most emotionally important topic of the past week that is significant for your actual situation or your future… Your therapist will answer your e-mail within 24 hours' (Wolf, Chung, & Kordy, 2010, p. 73). The study was designed as an intervention and the method was described as an 'email bridge' rather than a diary, but nevertheless the approach taken by researchers in this study shows the potential of email communication for diary-based researchers. Furthermore, it illustrates how different language can be used to describe the solicited diary method.

Another recent example of using email diary technique in social science research is an investigation into the impact on commuters of the London 2012 Olympic Games (Jones & Woolley, 2014). Twenty-three commuters were recruited to this study, which involved participants receiving an email asking them to produce a log of their journey, detailing anything they thought was different or significant, on each of the working days during the Olympics. The method achieved an 85 per cent completion rate (157 entries received) with eight of the diarists achieving 100 per cent completion (Jones & Woolley, 2014, p. 9). Clearly, then, email diary and digital communications more generally have the potential to add significant value to the researcher's methodological toolkit.

This brings us onto the topic of blogging – discrete 'posts' on the web usually written in chronological order by an individual. There is growing interest in the academic community about blogs, blogging and bloggers. Researchers are interested in the communication processes at work and the ways in which bloggers perform identity in blog entries. For example, Lee and Gretzel (2014) examined cross-cultural differences in travel blogs; Barker and Gill (2012) analysed levels of sexual subjectification in the Bitchy Jones diary blog; Blinka, Subrahmanyam, Smahel and Seganti (2012) compared the blogs of English-speaking and Czech-speaking teenagers; others have explored the ethics of blogging from the perspective of librarians (Powers, 2008) and examined the online identities of frequent bloggers (Bullingham & Vasconcelos, 2013). The phenomenon of video blogging has also been examined (Parker & Pfeiffer, 2005) and blogging has been used to create a research diary (Olive, 2012). All this illustrates how blogging has become a key communication tool for the digital age, with the practice itself becoming a well-documented research topic. But are bloggers diarists, and are the blogs they produce solicited diaries?

In Chapter 1, we outlined the difference between unsolicited and solicited diaries and emphasized that our focus in this text is on solicited diary method. We gave an example of a diary blog – the extract from a home care worker – and re-emphasized our interest in solicited diary method for research. However, blogging is akin to diary-writing and a common practice amongst proficient internet users. Arguably, this form of communication has re-energized and popularized the traditional form of diary keeping and might be regarded as the twenty-first-century equivalent of an unsolicited diary. The key difference is, of course, that online diarists – 'bloggers' – *are* writing for an audience to provoke debate and comments. The intended audience is unlikely to be a researcher, but an individual records his or her thoughts, feelings and activities in the blogosphere, *because* he or she wants others to read and engage with it. This differs from the traditional unsolicited diary that has never been intended for public use. Arguably, then, the boundaries between unsolicited and solicited diaries are becoming blurred and will continue to blur with the development of multi-author blogs and the proliferation of blogging. Clearly, blogs offer the diary researcher a potential source of data (Hookway, 2008). However, it is yet to be seen how these newest technologies can be utilized by diary researchers as data collection techniques.

Finally, it is noteworthy that researchers are increasingly using Facebook and other social media sites, because they provide publically accessible information about a person's life. As others in this series have discussed, online research is becoming increasingly prevalent as researchers discover that rich data can be collected via the internet (Hooley, Marriott, & Wellens, 2013). For instance, researchers have studied the extent to which health-care providers use social media sites (such as Facebook) in clinical practice to find out more about a patient (Jent et al., 2011). Similarly, there has been some work on the ethics of clinicians using Facebook to detect suicide ideations by clients with serious mental health problems (Lehavot, Ben-Zeev, & Neville, 2012). While these examples are neither diary-based studies nor concerned with solicited data, they do show how social media sites provide a time-structured digital platform for people to express their thoughts and feelings in a way that might be useful in a solicited diary-based study. Moreover, the information provided through these sites is not dissimilar to that gained through the Mass Observation Study – that is, it provides a useful glimpse into the everyday lives of people across Britain. Thus, it may be that it is used by researchers over time. Table 4.1 outlines the strengths and limitations of the range of technologies we have reviewed.

Table 4.1 Using technologies in diary research

Technology	Strengths	Limitations
Handheld electronic devices or personal digital assistants (PDAs)	Easy to use; convenient; questions can be programmed to suit participant Responses are unchangeable and verifiable, thus enhancing the quality and validity of data Costs of device can be set against no transcription costs and being able to reuse devices in future studies	Participants need to be confident, willing and able to use PDAs; might put some people off taking part in study Training required; this can vary from between five and twenty minutes Cost of equipment, including batteries and battery charger, can be expensive Technological problems – (re)charging batteries seems to be most common one – needs to be quickly resolved Habitual response style: participants may develop a tendency to rapidly skim over the questions without thinking about the actual experience
Capture technologies *General points applicable to all*	Effective way of collecting audiovisual information that moves beyond time-sequenced observation Certain participants (e.g. children and young people) seem to like it and are used to using these technologies Can take the researcher to places that would otherwise be prohibited, such as a boys' changing room, or unseen, such as a child's bedroom or working environment	Cost of equipment, including batteries and battery charger, can be expensive Some participants may find equipment difficult to use
Specific Photo diary using an analogue (disposable) camera	Easy to operate Restriction on amount of images that can be taken means that participants may give more thought and consideration to what to photograph	Delay between taking and seeing the photo can detract from enhancing behaviour change Hidden costs: processing images; having to drop off and collect camera; not very durable; so easily damaged, in which case replacement cameras may need to be purchased

Table 4.1 Continued

Technology	Strengths	Limitations
Photo diary using a digital camera	No restriction on amount of images that can be taken Photos can be uploaded onto a photo sharing (encrypted) website Allows participant to assess quality of images taken	Can produce too many images that are not relevant to study
Audio diary	Can be useful for gathering information that cannot always be captured using visual representation (e.g. an individual's thoughts or feelings) Can be used clandestinely in situations in which participants do not feel comfortable using a camera to photo an event (e.g. hospital or funeral)	Tend to produce longer transcripts so require more time and resources for transcription and analysis
Mobile phone diary	Easy for participants to use and integrate into lifestyle; no need for training; generates data that it is easy to store and manage Able to control accuracy of recording; user-friendly	Not possible to use mobile phone in some settings (e.g. cinema, while driving, clinical areas) If participants have to use their own mobile phone, there is a risk they exceed their limit and incur personal costs Potential for making mistakes if have to answer large number of questions
Voice-mail diary study technique	Built-in features (such as play and pause and restarting) are useful for transcription Able to review diary entries on submission, rather than seeing them all at the end of the study	There is limited recording time with voice-mail Diffidence amongst people about speaking into a voice recorder.
Internet-based (e.g. email and blogs)	The process can be monitored better; if someone is keeping an online diary, it is potentially easier for the researcher to 'drop in' and see if the participant needs additional guidance or support	Success of the project may depend on having a good IT support team, which can be costly

(Continued)

Table 4.1 Continued

Technology	Strengths	Limitations
	Provides the opportunity for immediate interviews and personalized feedback, which can enhance communication between the researcher and participant	Access to the internet may be a problem for some participants
	Printable diary pages can be used as a back-up plan for people who may not have access to the internet	

Research areas where technologies are embraced or have potential application

There are several areas of research where technologies are being embraced and regularly used to collect data. One of these is health care. Electronic diaries have become a well-established methodology in clinical research, for both tracking symptoms or behaviours and empirically testing clinical and theoretical hypotheses (Connelly & Bickel, 2011). This is evidenced by various pieces of work including a systematic review of the effectiveness of using electronic diaries in pain and symptom research (Burton et al., 2007) and a review on the benefits of using electronic diaries to gain a fuller assessment of clients in their own environments (Piasecki & Hufford, 2007). Health researchers and clinicians realize the potential of electronic diaries and integrate the method into study designs.

Research with children is another area where technologies are embraced. Researchers recognize that today's children and young people have grown up with digital media and electronic means of communication and are used to using them, or at least be accustomed to the concept of recording oneself or using an electronic device. For example, Noyes (2004, p. 197) assumed that the children in his video-diary study would be familiar with the idea of a video-diary room from the TV programme *Big Brother*. As well as it being a familiar process, video-diary method is particularly well suited to child research as it allows for a freer form of self-expression and advanced writing and language skills are not required (Buchwald, 2009). It is perhaps not surprising, therefore, that the majority of studies which use digital technologies involve children or young people. Children and young people are the digital generation (Buckingham & Willett, 2006).

A third research area to embrace the use of technologies in diary-based research is disability studies. Researchers value the flexibility that technologies can provide and will use and integrate a range of approaches to enable the participation of people with a disability in research. We have identified two studies which have used digital technologies with people with a disability (Bartlett, 2012; Worth, 2009); there are many other studies within the disability field that use technologies, including, for example, a photographic study involving adults with learning disability (Aldridge, 2007). While these are not diary-designed studies, they do illustrate their potential for integrating into diary-based studies with different groups of people.

Hence, as well as discussing the research areas where technologies are being used, it is worthwhile identifying those areas where they have some potential application, but are not currently deployed. For example, it is perhaps surprising that audio diaries have not been used to study changes in speech and language, especially in health-related research where such changes can signify worsening or improving health (as is the case with dementia or stroke). Similarly, electronic diaries or mobile phone technologies could be used more frequently within the fields of gerontology and geriatric medicine to investigate, for example, intergenerational changes in family dynamics in the wake of a household member being diagnosed with an age-related condition like dementia, type 2 diabetes or age-related macular degeneration. Digital diary methods would allow researchers to gain contextual/numerical/situational information within which the experience occurs, to inform health and social care practice. They can also provide participants with an alternative means of expression beyond the standard interview.

Questions to consider before using technology

There are many practical, ethical, methodological and epistemological issues to consider when using technologies in diary-based research. Some of these have been alluded to in this chapter, and they are important to highlight and summarize, in order to provide a helpful reference point for both new and experienced researchers. Drawing on the studies reviewed, we have created some core questions, see table 4.2 below, that can usefully be considered before incorporating digital technologies in your research design.

Table 4.2 Questions to consider before using digital technologies

---

1. Is the technology appropriate for your research area and question?

2. Are participants used to using the technology, or will training be required?

3. Does the technology suit the needs of the participant?

4. How will you respond to any technical problems?

5. Do you have the knowledge and skills to deal with any technical problems?

6. If using a mobile phone or other ubiquitous form of technology, will you issue participants with the device or allow them to use their own?

7. Have you allowed time for developing and piloting the technology?

8. How might the technology affect the research relationship?

9. Have other researchers used the same technology with the same population? If so, what can you learn from their oversights or slip-ups? If not, how do you feel about breaking new methodological ground?

Conclusion

In this chapter, we have considered the ways in which technologies are changing the nature of diary keeping and impacting on diary-based research. We have highlighted the rise of computerized or electronic diaries, the growing use of capture technologies such as video cameras and how researchers are beginning to use the internet, emails and blogs in diary-based research. The advantages and limitations of these technologies have been identified and discussed. In particular, we have highlighted some of the conditions when it might be better to use technologies over paper-based methods.

Finally, however innovative and novel the use of technologies in diary-based research may seem to us now, they will not be to the next generation of researchers. Our approach to photo diaries will need to change, as digital cameras become redundant with the arrival of devices such as smartphones and tablets. In addition, other 'technological advances will supersede the mobile phone method in time' (Plowman & Stevenson, 2012, p. 550). Furthermore, advances in wearable technologies and development of miniature sensors, which clinicians are already capitalizing on to gather key data (see, e.g., Bonato, 2005) might well pave the way for a whole new mode of diary-based research. Clearly, changes in technology are constant, rapid and likely to impact or influence on our lives in unpredictable ways, especially when it comes to using technologies in diary-based research. The scholarly literature struggles to keep pace with the methodological issues facing researchers.

5 Exploring issues of participation, control and ethics

Introduction

This chapter focuses on issues of empowerment, control and research ethics in the context of diary keeping. At the heart of discussion is the question, To what extent can diary techniques help to nurture equitable research relations? Equitable research relations can be defined as a relationship concerned with knowledge construction in which both parties (researcher and participant) share control of the process. Developing equitable relations is becoming increasingly important in social and health-related research as more emphasis is placed on conducting research *with* rather than *on* people. Our concern in this chapter is how diary keeping can help or hinder this endeavour.

Building on the practical issues previously discussed in this book, the chapter commences by explaining what it means to use diary method in a participatory way before examining the positive effects of diary keeping and the key advantages of diary method over interviews. While recognizing some of the limitations of diary techniques, we suggest that the main strengths of diary methods (particularly exploratory and unstructured approaches) are that they provide research participants with greater control over the pace and nature of data collection compared to the more traditional techniques of interviewing. In discussing these issues, the chapter will examine how diary method can be modified and tailored for different research groups, including vulnerable populations. Hence, we suggest that diary method is a potentially useful tool for building equitable relations between researcher and participant because it affords the participant more control over data collection.

The chapter also acknowledges that there are several limitations with diary method, most notably that it relies on research participants having the motivation, skills, intellect, time and capacity to maintain a diary over a defined period of time. Additionally, the process of keeping a diary can have negative effects, such as drawing attention to family conflicts and the repetitive nature of everyday life. These strengths and limitations will be illustrated by drawing on examples from real-world research.

Using diary method in a participatory way: Building equitable relations

In recent years, there has been a growing trend in social and health-related research to develop data collection methods which enable participants to articulate their experiences. Rather than focusing primarily on the needs of the research project, researchers are prioritizing and developing techniques which also empower participants in some way. This might mean, for example, involving research participants in the design of a study and/or using tools of data collection which enable participants to have greater control over the research process. Collectively, these approaches are known as participatory methods.

Participatory approaches involve the researcher working with participants in a respectful and engaging way. It involves a high degree of accountability and responsibility towards the research participants. The difference between participatory and non-participatory approaches is essentially one of power. For instance, historically there has been a massive imbalance of power between researchers and people with disabilities (Stone & Priestley, 1996). Such an imbalance is still evident within dementia research where researchers will use the Mini Mental State Examination or other measures to assess the ability of a person with dementia to participate in a study, even though individuals with this condition may find this a humiliating experience (Hellström, Nolan, Nordenfelt, & Lundh, 2007). The goal in participatory research, however, is to develop equitable relations between researchers and participants and to conduct research which involves and benefits participants in some way.

Several researchers seek to use diary method in a participatory way. Typically, these studies are related to health-care services or involve bringing about institutional change. For example, Elg et al. (2011) used solicited diaries to involve patients in the development of health-care services and suggest that diaries 'become a voice for patients in the health care system' (140). For this study, participants were asked to write about everyday situations based on their own health experiences and then write down ideas for improvement based on their experiences. Fourteen diaries containing a total of 102 ideas for improvement were created (Elg et al., 2011). As such, the diaries provided a conduit for voicing discontent and empowered patients to express their opinions about how to improve services.

The channelling nature of diary method lends itself well to participatory approaches. Participants can express themselves freely and honestly in a diary, especially a video diary, which offers the opportunity to use spoken language. For example, researchers who have used video diary with younger people have found that once the children got over the initial strangeness of talking to an anonymous video camera, the process helped them to clarify their thoughts and feelings (Buchwald, 2009). As such, keeping a (video) diary becomes beneficial for the participant, as well as the researcher. We will return to this point later in this chapter.

The positive effects of diary keeping

In this section, we consider how the act of diary keeping can have a potentially positive effect on participants. The effects we identify and discuss, including affording participants choice and control, affording participants time, providing an outlet for difficult thoughts and feelings and raising awareness of positive things, might be regarded as the strengths of diary-method in respect of building equitable relations.

Affording participants choice and control

Several researchers report that solicited diary method affords participants greater control over the data collection process (Bijoux & Myers, 2006). There are several reasons for this. Firstly, the flexibility of the method often makes it easier for participants to fit data collection into their everyday life. For example, a study of breast-feeding difficulties amongst first-time mothers used audio diaries, as information could be provided when convenient for the participant and in their home environment (Williamson et al., 2012). Similarly, mobile audio diaries were used in a study of commuter cycling: participants provided an account of their experiences of commuting on a bicycle while actually doing it (Jones, 2012). In both cases, participants (and not the researcher) were ultimately in control over the pace and time of data collection.

Related to the above, diary method affords more choice and control to participants in terms of how much information to provide. Unlike interview method, where researchers are typically schooled to prompt participants if the conversation dries up, diary method allows people to disclose as much, or as little as they like. For instance, it is common in paper-based diary studies for some entries to be just a few lines, whereas others run to a few pages (see, e.g., Keleher & Verrinder, 2003). Similarly, in a video-diary study involving over seventy young girls, the researchers suggested ten minutes a day, but most girls filmed less frequently and for longer (Jackson & Vares, 2013). As diary researchers note, participants will keep their diaries in their own way, and the 'power of selection is handed over to the participant' (Bijoux & Myers, 2006, p. 51).

Secondly, diary method affords participants greater control over how their lives and experiences are represented. Even though guidance is provided, a participant may choose to disregard this and express themselves in their own way. One diary-based study by Gibson (2002) involved young men with a physical disability keeping audio and photo diaries; four participants, however, chose to use the added function of the camera to include videos without any instruction to do so (p. 12). Similarly, in a study exploring the effect of participation in adapted cycling on quality of life for children with cerebral palsy, one of the young participants chose to draw a picture of her bike in her written diary (Pickering, Horrocks, Visser, & Todd, 2013). Both of these studies show how diary method can offer participants greater choice and control over the data they choose to give; plus, it provides further evidence of how diary method can put the researched, rather than researcher, in control of data gathering.

Thirdly, video and audio diaries provide participants with editorial control. The participant is in charge of the on/off switch and can normally delete recordings whenever he or she chooses. For instance, in Bartlett's study one man with dementia who kept an audio diary could be heard taking his time to find the right word (he would say "worm" instead of "word") and he switched the recorder on and off (presumably to prepare to speak) (Bartlett, 2012). In this instance, the method afforded the participant both the time and freedom to edit his own data. Having control over data production in this way is linked to more equitable research relations (Roberts, 2011). Moreover, it offers a way for individuals who may otherwise be excluded (or exclude themselves) from participating in a study without feeling pressurized or unable to contribute.

Fourthly, when diary method is used as part of a suite of data collected tools, it gives participants a flexible option as to how to relay information.

We all have preferred styles of communication, it therefore makes sense to offer participants different ways to convey information about themselves and/or the phenomenon under investigation. For example, in one investigation into risk and worry in everyday life, research participants were given the choice of keeping a diary (for one week) or taking part in an interview (Hawkes, Houghton, & Rowe, 2009). Other researchers who have used diary method regretted not giving participants more choice about being able to include pre-existing photographs in their data (Gibson, 2002). Thus, diary method affords both the researcher and participant considerable flexibility to protect the welfare of participants.

Affording participants time

Another way in which diaries can be empowering is by affording participants more time to collect their thoughts and feelings than a standard interview allows. Rather than having to respond immediately to questions or others talking (as is the case with individual and group interviews), the diary provides a mechanism for participants to prepare what they want to say at their own pace and in their own time (Gibson, 2002). For instance, focus groups and diaries were used in one study exploring South African women's experiences of violence, and at least one participant preferred the latter method. She said, 'I found it better to write than talk during the focus group because I wrote at my own pace. There was no rush. I had time to memorise' (Meth, 2003, p. 200). Having the time to compose one's response can be experienced as enabling by some people, which maybe a particularly important feature when involving people with an impairment or illness that may affect their capacity to respond straightaway to data collection questions.

The temporality of data collection is not always considered in the context of research methods, but it can be an important factor in the enabling process. Asking people to report on something as near as possible to the time that something happened is much easier for the participant; plus, it will capture more accurate data and help mitigate against recall bias. Researchers recognized this when investigating the recurrence of pain in children, sending text messages to children at fixed time intervals during the day (Alfvén, 2010). An SMS message was sent to the child six times a day with the simple question: Have you had pain? If they had, they were asked to rate the pain on a scale of 1 to 5. The researchers found this to be an effective method for investigating the recurrence of pain amongst young children, especially as children had to remember whether they had pain only during the last three hours. In this case, the relatively short time frame enabled participants to report their experiences more accurately and placed less demands on them to recall and remember events.

Providing an outlet for difficult thoughts and feelings

Another way in which diary method can be empowering is by providing an outlet for participants to work through difficult thoughts and feelings. Several researchers highlight the potential therapeutic value of diary keeping for participants in this regard. This was exemplified in one study of midwifery practices, where the research team found that the act of keeping a written diary provided an outlet for midwives to address stressful situations and find solutions to complex problems (Bedwell, McGowan, & Lavender, 2012). In another study investigating the transition from medical student to junior doctor, one respondent reported that the process of keeping an audio diary helped him to 'unburden' himself from the stressful situations that had occurred that day (Brennan et al., 2010). Obviously other methods, such as repeated interviews, may offer a similar benefit, but diary method is arguably a more useful channel due to the immediacy of the encounter (with the diary) and the structure it provides.

The traditional mode of diary keeping (i.e. writing) provides a structured space for self-expression and reflection. Indeed, it has been found that the process of writing can be beneficial for people with health problems, for it allows individuals to 'release complex emotions by naming them ... and work their way through the many changes in their daily lives' (Ryan, 2006, p. 423). This is certainly what the following researchers found in their diary studies:

- involving family caregivers of people with dementia; participants said they found the process of writing diary entries therapeutic because it helped them to express their frustrations and think more clearly about the situation they were in Välimäki, Vehviläinen-Julkunen, and Pietilä (2007);
- about living with HIV/Aids in Namibia; participants told the researchers they found the diary-keeping process therapeutic because it made them feel their opinions were valued (Thomas, 2007);
- involving older people living with cancer; participants said they found 'keeping a diary a helpful outlet' (Richardson, 1994, p. 786).

Clearly, a diary provides a useful space for ventilating difficult thoughts and feelings, especially when that person is ill or facing adversity.

All this said, diary writing may be experienced by some as either challenging or constraining. As other researchers have pointed out, diary writing requires good literacy skills and command of the (English) language; moreover, we are schooled to write in a structured way and to produce written texts which are highly organized and linear (Roberts, 2011). For some individuals, especially children and those with lower educational abilities, this may not be easy. In this case a written diary is unlikely to provide a helpful outlet for self-expression, in fact it may even pose a risk to a participant's emotional well-being by highlighting something that they are unable to do. Fortunately, the *written* diary is not the only mode of diary available to researchers.

Visual diaries are becoming an increasingly popular method of data collection, especially in research involving children and young adults. There seems to be a growing consensus within the childhood research community that video diaries (and visual methods more generally) can enable children and young people to express themselves more honestly and spontaneously than traditional research methods (Noyes, 2009). In particular, video diaries can provide a useful outlet for young people to deal with difficult emotions and patterns of thinking. For example, in one study involving children keeping a video diary, one participant who said he usually found it difficult to talk about his feelings of anger told the researcher that the video diary had helped him to overcome the problem (Buchwald, 2009). In another study, the video camera became the only 'person' one young participant could talk to; it acted as a confidante and, as such, provided an outlet for this child to talk about the problems she was having at school (Noyes, 2004). For participants who find writing a challenge, the medium of video provides a potentially more effective mode of expression.

Raising awareness of positive things

Another way in which diary keeping can be empowering is by raising participants' awareness of positive things. Several research papers describe how the process of recording routine activities can make participants more aware of what is actually happening in their life, which they found beneficial. For example, the self-recording of daily activities related to falls and fear of falling increased participants' awareness of risky behaviours they were previously unaware of (Bailey, Foran, Ni Scanaill, & Dromey, 2011). Similarly, in a study of online privacy, which involved weekly diary entries for ten weeks, participants said that taking part had 'increased their level of awareness and sensitivity towards on-line privacy and consent issues, as well as altering the behaviour' (Bogdanovic, Dowd, Wattam, & Adam, 2012, p. 218). In another small-scale study involving two married working mothers, participants reported becoming more aware of switching from one task to another through the diary-writing process (Orban et al., 2012). Clearly, looking back over diary entries, or knowing that you need to make one later in the day, heightens a person's awareness of everyday habits.

Some researchers consciously use diary method to raise awareness. Such an approach is perhaps most common in health-related research where a change in a person's behaviour is desired. For example, Zepeda and Deal (2008) used photographic and written food diaries in an attempt to raise awareness amongst participants about what they eat and to alter dietary attitudes. They found it an effective method as 'the immediacy of the camera forced reflection at the point of consumption' (p. 696). In another study, researchers asked eight people diagnosed with schizophrenia to keep a food diary, partly to educate this population about healthy eating (Hardy & Gray, 2012). Food diaries are a good example of how diary method might be used as an intervention to raise awareness and achieve positive outcomes.

More often than not, though, it is not the intention of the researcher to raise participants' awareness. Researchers tend to report it is an unexpected outcome resulting from using diary method. For example, in the diary-interview study involving thirteen basketball players, a few participants said in their post-diary interview how the diary-keeping process helped to raise their awareness of their most effective coping strategies (Tamminen & Holt, 2010). In this instance, diary keeping benefits the participant (as well as the researcher) by providing an opportunity for individuals to reflect on their everyday practices.

Several researchers report that the process of keeping a diary helped participants become extra mindful of the everyday things they do at work. There are numerous examples of professionals learning from the diary-writing experience. For instance, in one study, school teachers were asked to maintain a classroom diary to explore patterns of learning and teaching and found the process of diary keeping useful. As the researchers note, '[D]iary writing and the permanent process of analysis and reflection that writing induces, causes regularities, patterns and theoretical insights to arise in the researcher's mind' (Informa et al., 2010, p. 166). Likewise, in another study involving parents and nursery staff observing and recording children's mood and play patterns, researchers reported how participants said they learnt a lot about the value of observing children at play and found the experience of diary keeping an educational and interesting one (Lämsä, Rönkä, Poikonen, & Malinen, 2012). Also, in a study exploring midwives' experiences of intrapartum care, researchers reported how the process encouraged some participants to reflect more than usual on everyday clinical practices (Bedwell et al., 2012). Clearly, diary method can benefit some participants by enhancing professional practices.

The negative effects of diary keeping

In this section, we turn to the potentially negative effects of diary keeping on participants. The effects we identify and discuss, including respondent fatigue, over-disclosure and raising awareness of negative things, might be regarded as the limitations of diary method in respect of building equitable relations.

Respondent fatigue

Respondent fatigue is a well-documented limitation of diary method, which we have referred to already in this book. Essentially this is when participants tire of keeping their diary, and entries become more sporadic or tail off completely. For example, Jacelon and Imperio (2005) invited a group of community-dwelling older adults to keep a diary about how they managed their chronic health problems for two weeks. They found that participants begun to tire of making entries during the second week. As one of the participants commented, 'keeping a diary was interesting in the beginning, then it got to be a bore' (p. 994). Similarly, in another study involving older people keeping a diary for a two-week period, the researchers noticed a decline in the detail of entries after week one (Johnson & Bytheway, 2001). However, it would be wrong to take from this that respondent fatigue is due to age or infirmity, as younger people may find diary keeping tiresome too. Respondent fatigue seems to be a potential hazard of diary method, regardless of the participant group.

Diary method is not inherently fatiguing and burdensome. It depends on how it is used, the methodological approach taken by the researchers and to some extent the circumstances in which the participant lives and their feelings about keeping a diary. For example, people living in low-income countries may well regard diary keeping as a 'waste of time' and unnecessary distraction from essential chores (Meth, 2003, p. 203). In other situations, participants may find the process of keeping a diary more demanding than expected, as was the case with participants in a Finnish study of everyday activities in a children's nursery (Lämsä et al., 2012). Even though it was for only one week, participants complained at the end about having to complete it each morning.

The demands of diary keeping can mean that some people do not complete their diaries. For example, the researchers investigating medication use in older people estimated that between five and ten per cent of (potential) participants were put off or dropped out because of the diary method (Johnson & Bytheway, 2001). In another study on running away amongst Hmong girls, ironically one of the participants ran away before completing her diary (Edinburgh et al., 2013). As discussed in Chapter 3, where dropout becomes too large in a study, it can have some serious implications for data analysis and the veracity of the findings.

Over-disclosure

Another potentially negative effect of diary keeping is that it can encourage over-disclosure. There is something about the act of diary keeping that encourages participants to reveal their innermost thoughts and feelings when they might not want to or have to for the research project. As one researcher, who used audio diary with new medical students, noted, the method can create an 'intimate association; one in which participants feel comfortable to share their most difficult and intense experiences' (Monrouxe, 2009, p. 8). This is certainly what one of us found when one of the participants discussed his marital problems in the audio diary (Bartlett, 2012). Others may become extremely anxious at the prospect of having to keep a diary that other people will see (Johnson & Bytheway, 2001) – possibly because they fear over-disclosing. Over-disclosure is more likely in an unstructured (rather than structured) diary design and is a particularly important consideration with vulnerable research participants, such as young children, who may have trouble controlling their emotions when making a diary entry (Buchwald, 2009).

Raising awareness of negative things

Diary keeping can raise awareness of negative things, too. As researchers who have used diary methods to research marital relationships point out, the process of diary keeping 'may increase awareness of the strengths of a marital relationship, or it may lead to awareness and rumination about conflict or relationship weakness' (Laurenceau & Bolger, 2005, p. 95). This is what Thomas (2006) found in her research into the stigma of living with HIV/Aids in Namibia, which involved asking seven ill people and their main carer to keep a diary for between one and six months. Some participants' diary entries revealed a certain degree of conflict between family members. Thus, she noted, 'because diaries are recorded in the private sphere of the household, it is not possible to know how their recording might have impacted upon intra-household tensions' (p. 3174). It is imperative, therefore, that researchers consider the potential impact of a person keeping a diary on their family when designing and recruiting participants to a diary-based study.

Other researchers have found that the process of keeping a diary can raise awareness of the repetitive and mundane nature of a person's life. In fact, both of us found this in our respective studies involving family carers (Milligan et al., 2005) and adults with dementia (Bartlett, 2012). In Milligan's study with carers of frail older people, at least one participant found that the act of diary keeping made her aware for the first time of how repetitive and boring her life was, a factor she had not previously thought about. Similarly, one participant told Bartlett (2012), that he had not written much in his diary, and what he had recorded he thought it was 'all very boring ... I get up and clean the house, blah blah' is how he described some of his entries in his post-diary interview. While the researcher may find such minutiae useful or significant, he or she should be aware that the participant may experience the recording of it as irksome.

Researchers should also be aware that some participants may be put off taking part in a study if they are asked to keep a diary, because it raises awareness of negative things. People may not want to routinely record certain aspects of their lifestyle. For example, one team of clinical researchers reported an 'unexpectedly high rate of refusal to participate' in their study using food diaries to manage obesity (Gregory et al., 2006, p. 68). It might have been that people did not want to be reminded of their weight and/ or food consumption. Similarly, in an internet-based diary study, which involved 1765 participants giving a brief description of an event and rating its frequency and significance, 25 per cent of the sample dropped out after the first stage. Significantly, those who dropped out had on average a lower level of education than the group who completed the study (Kristo, Janssen, & Murre, 2009). In this case, keeping a diary may have reminded participants of their low expressive skills.

One aspect of diary keeping that can make it demanding for participants is a lack of control over when diary entries are made. If the researcher (rather than the participant) is in charge of this aspect of diary keeping, participants may be more likely to find the process onerous. Take, for example, the Finnish study mentioned earlier; participants were required to complete a structured diary sheet at a particular time each day (in the morning); there was no flexibility to record events in the evening, which is when participants would have preferred to have done it (the researchers discovered this at the end) (Lämsä et al., 2012). Other researchers note that diaries can become intrusive when participants are required to complete entries at random time intervals (Bolger et al., 2003). Thus, affording participants no control over the timing of diary entries can make the method more onerous.

The significance of affording participants control has been discussed previously. However, we want to return to it in the context of protecting the welfare of participants, as although participants may have control *during* the diary-keeping process, it is typically relinquished as soon as the diary is collected by the researcher. As these midwifery researchers have astutely pointed out, 'by handing over a document the writer loses control and may feel vulnerable. In addition, the participant cannot know what the researcher's reaction to it will be' (Bedwell et al., 2012, p. 153). Similarly, when it comes to data analysis, 'the choice of which data to include and the interpretation of the data is in the power of the adult researcher' (Punch, 2002, p. 329). In particular, being filmed has been associated with a loss of control, possibly because individuals fear they may be recognized or that recordings might go astray (Flewitt, 2006). Ultimately, the researcher is in control of the project.

Using diary method cautiously and flexibly with 'vulnerable' populations

Traditionally, researchers have sought to comply with rigid methodological procedures. This has meant adhering to standard scientific practices rather than using methods flexibly to suit the needs and interests of participants. In researching this book, we noticed that research papers dated pre-1990 were more likely to use expressions like 'standard day diary' and be concerned with adhering to positivist principles (e.g. Lawson, Robinson, & Bakes, 1985). There was very little, if any, emphasis on flexibility to enable research participation or concern for taking a participatory approach. While rigid adherence to standard methodological principles may be unproblematic in some research contexts, it is rarely appropriate when conducting research with 'vulnerable' people and/or in vulnerable research environments.

The term 'vulnerable' is often used in an uncritical way by policymakers and the research community to refer to specific individuals, groups or settings, as outlined below. Research ethics committee members and research funders use official understandings of vulnerability like this to guide their decision-making and protocols, which in turn determines the way researchers can recruit and involve people in their studies. A researcher may find it particularly hard to get ethical permission to recruit people with dementia to their study, for example, because people with this condition have been classified as 'vulnerable'. However, official definitions of vulnerability are problematic and while they might seem 'value-free on closer inspection they are value-laden' (Brown, 2011, p. 318).

The term 'vulnerable' is generally held to refer to those individuals or groups who, due to age, ill-health, disability or minority status, may be open to exploitation (whether physical, emotional or psychological). This would include, for example, children, adults with learning disabilities and progressive health conditions such as dementia and Parkinson's disease and people with physical disabilities. People can also be vulnerable simply by virtue of the group they belong to (or to which others consider them to belong) especially if that group is stigmatized or marginalized. Examples include asylum seekers, Romany travellers and ethnic and religious minorities. Individuals may also be vulnerable through being part of an institution. This is complex. Institutional membership may carry social stigma; moreover being institutionalized can diminish autonomy, thereby making people vulnerable; and both these aspects can interact with personal 'vulnerabilities' that brought the individual into the institution in the first place.

Quoted from Social Science Research Ethics page http://www.lancaster.ac.uk/researchethics/4-2-understandings.html

From a methodological perspective, official constructions of vulnerability are problematic on several counts. First, those classified as vulnerable might not be exploited, stigmatized or marginalized, and may even take offence to the idea that others think they have 'special needs' and require extra protection. As Brown (2012) notes, this is certainly one of the objections disability rights activists have about the blanket use of 'vulnerability' in relation to people with a disability. Second, it is assumed that vulnerability is an inherently negative position or weakness; it could, however, be conceptualized as 'openness, susceptibility, and receptiveness' (Wiles, 2011, p. 573). Third, by naming certain individuals and settings as vulnerable, there is a danger that other people and situations (not named) are also vulnerable but not seen as such. It is therefore important that the term 'vulnerability' is used with caution, as it may not adequately capture a person's experience or situation.

Flexibility is increasingly seen as an essential aspect of qualitative research within the health field where participants are often ill, impaired or in pain (Thorne, 2011). Typically, this means adapting a method to enable a group of participants to use it and/or ensuring it is appropriate for a particular setting. For instance, in one study, primary school children were asked to complete a 'picture-based symptom diary' because some participants had yet to learn to read (Lundqvist, Rugland, Clench-Aas, Bartonova, & Hofoss, 2010). Similarly, pictorial diaries were used in a Gambian-based study because researchers knew participants would have low literacy skills (Wiseman et al., 2005). These examples show how researchers need to be flexible and creative if they want to maximize the variety of individuals and settings in their research.

Finally, it is important to highlight the 'situated ethics' that surround diary method, particularly photo and video diaries, which can be more public in process and form than written or audio diaries. Situated ethics are those which are contextual and cannot be foreseen by the researcher (Wiles, 2012). For instance, in a small-scale study exploring the meaning of a 'welcoming community' to adults with learning disability, one male participant told researchers in a follow-up interview that he was questioned about what he was doing by a passer-by while standing in a street taking photographs of the house he used to live in as a child (Power & Bartlett, 2015). Participants may want to take photographs or make video recordings of other people or meaningful places; this process can place them in a potentially vulnerable or even dangerous situation.

A common ethical dilemma in diary-based studies, especially those involving visual methods, is protecting the identity of participants, as well as others who are included in diaries. As Nicholl (2010, p. 20) points out, 'when designing a diary study, it is important to plan for confidentiality, not only for the participant but for others who may be included in recordings'. This might mean, for example, obscuring the faces of individuals in photographs or instructing participants not to take images of certain people or places. However, this in itself raises ethical issues; as such practices and directives may affront and/or place undue demands on the participant (Wiles, 2013).

Several researchers have modified the diary method to make it more suitable for young children, older adults or people with disabilities. Modifications might be made to a particular form of diary keeping or to standard conventions associated with diary keeping. For example, Lillegaard, Løken, and Andersen (2007) designed a pre-coded food diary to help children complete their diary sheets. In another study on the use of medication in later life involving older people, most of whom were aged seventy-five years and over, the researchers told participants to invite someone else to scribe if they felt unable to write their own diary (Johnson & Bytheway, 2001). Other researchers have suggested that separate diary designs are a good idea for younger children and adolescents (O'Donnell, Marshman, & Zaitoun, 2013). Sensitivity to a person's situation, age and abilities is key here; simple changes to standard methodological practices and procedures can mean a wider range of people can participate. In addition, such changes can help to protect the autonomy and dignity of participants.

Individuals have different educational backgrounds and priorities; it is perhaps inevitable, then, that some people will feel more comfortable than others sharing information about themselves with a researcher via a written diary. Thus, even though modifications might be made to the diary method, 'the voices of all participants may not be heard equally' if due consideration is not given to a person's educational background or situation (Koopman-Boyden & Richardson, 2013, p. 398).

Ethical considerations with diary method

As with all research methods, there are ethical issues to consider when designing a study and collecting data. It is beyond the scope of this short text to discuss research ethics in any substantial detail, besides which, one of the books published in this series is concerned with ethical issues in research, and we would direct the reader to this text for a more detailed account (Wiles, 2013). Our intention in this section is to identify and briefly discuss the most salient ethical issues around using diary methods, especially video diaries and photo diaries, which raise particularly challenging issues related to privacy, anonymity and confidentiality.

Ensuring privacy

The issue of privacy is a particularly salient one in relation to diary method, especially video diaries. Participants will want to know that what they say on camera cannot be overheard by other people in another room. In one video-diary study involving year 6 school children, the young participants wanted to know exactly where the video camera was going to be set up in the school as they did not want anything they said on camera to be overheard by other pupils or teachers (Noyes, 2004). Other researchers have given participants the choice of where to keep their video diary in an effort to promote a sense of privacy (Edinburgh et al., 2013).

Privacy is an issue with written diaries, too. Participants may be concerned about where to store their diary during the diary-keeping phase so that others do not read it. This might be a real concern in diary studies about sensitive topics such as sexual behaviour. In fact, Minnis and Padian (2001) asked young participants in their study of adolescent sexual behaviour where they kept their written diaries and found the commonly cited location for storing the diary calendars was a "secret" bedroom drawer (39 per cent). Privacy may be a particular issue, then, in an institutional setting, such as a care home, hospital or prison, where others may have easy access to a person's belongings and/or personal spaces may be limited. It may also be an issue for people with a visual or cognitive impairment or other disability (such as a learning disability), who may require some assistance when making diary entries. In such circumstances, it would be important for the researcher to discuss and record where the participant would like to store their diary during the consent process, so this information can be relayed to the person's assistant if they have one.

Providing financial incentives

The use of financial incentives can be a contentious topic in research. Offering people money to participate in a study raises several resource and methodological issues. Not least of these is that it may induce someone to take part, especially if payment is offered to those who might be considered economically vulnerable (Tishler & Bartholomae, 2002). However, as nurse researchers have pointed out, 'providing financial incentives is not morally problematic. Simply based on respect, it seems fair that participants receive some compensation in exchange for their time and associated burden' (Ulrich & Grady, 2004, p. 73). Clearly, financial incentives have a role to play in encouraging people to take part in research and there is an increasing recognition, certainly amongst research funders and within the diary methods community more specifically, that some compensation should be offered, especially where considerable time and effort is required of the participant.

Judgements about whether or not it is a good or bad idea to use financial incentives are complex and beyond the scope of this short text. So, rather than discussing the pros and cons of providing financial incentives, we thought it more helpful to outline a selection of diary-based studies that have used monetary incentives (see Table 5.1). In this way, it becomes possible to see how financial incentives have been used in diary studies, the different amounts that people have been paid and the effects of using financial incentives. With this information, the reader can form his or her own opinion about the merits of providing financial incentives to participants involved in a diary-based study.

Table 5.1 Using financial incentives in diary studies

Study	Amount	Response rate
Fifty-four respondents directly affected by the 2001 foot and mouth disease epidemic in rural Cumbria maintained a weekly diary for eighteen months (Mort et al., 2005)	Each diarist received £10 per week every four weeks on collection of their diaries (£40 per visit)	Diary writing began in the week of 21 December and continued over the next eighteen months, during which time just three respondents chose to discontinue. Periods of "holiday" from diary writing were negotiated, and the total number of weekly diaries collected (at monthly visits to the diarists) was 3071

(Continued)

Table 5.1 Continued

Study	Amount	Response rate
Forty-six non-professional dual-earner couples made diary entries every evening using a personal digital assistant (electronic diary) for a two-week period (Bass, Linney, Butler, & Grzywacz, 2007)	Each couple received $100 for their time	Fifty-three participants had records for all fourteen days and eighty-two participants had ten or more observations. Due to missing evaluation data, three couples were dropped from the study
Seventy-five heterosexual students (forty-four women, thirty-one men) made daily recordings of sexual behaviour, condom use and alcohol or substance use for one month (Graham, Catania, Brand, Duong, & Canchola, 2003)	Compensation for the diary phase was paid at a follow-up visit, as follows: $1.00 for each diary completed and mailed back on a daily basis, for a total of $28.00 at the end of four weeks	Sixty-nine participants (forty-one females, twenty-eight males) completed the study
Participants completed an internet-based structured weekly sex diary for six weeks. The men were asked to complete a survey each week on the same day, with a grace period of three days (Boone et al., 2013)	Each participant was paid $20 for baseline measure, and between $5 and $15 for each subsequent online survey completed. The incentive structure was a progressive one, with participants earning larger amounts the longer they stayed in the study (p. 1884)	There was a 78 per cent response rate across the six weeks of the structured diary, with response rates for individual weeks ranging from 77 to 88 per cent
This randomized controlled study included 105 sexually active female adolescents aged 15–19 years, recruited from amongst teens seeking reproductive health-care services at a family planning clinic in the San Francisco Bay Area.	All study participants received $35 reimbursement for interviews and for completing the diary compared with the requirements of the written diary; additional opportunities to earn small incentives for completing the diary daily were integrated into the telephone protocol.	Fifty-two per cent of participants completed twenty-one or more days of the 28-day diary period, with over one-third of those completing the diary every day

Table 5.1 Continued

Study	Amount	Response rate
Participants completed a standardized sexual behaviour diary questionnaire each day for four weeks (Minnis & Padian, 2001)	As an incentive to complete the diary, participants received one ticket into a monthly gift certificate drawing for each diary calendar they returned or each telephone call they made. In addition, small prizes were given to respondents who either phoned the diary on two randomly selected incentive days each week or returned their written diary calendar for a randomly selected week each month	The most important reason for diary completion was the opportunity to earn the incentives disbursed for randomly selected days on which diary data were reported

Conclusion

In this penultimate chapter, we have considered the extent to which diary method can help to nurture equitable research relations between researchers and participants. We have explored the drawbacks of this method as well as its strengths and discussed the extent to which it affords participants choice and control over the reporting of their lives. On balance we would argue that if diary method is used flexibly, with care and according to high ethical standards, it can certainly help to nurture equitable relations, especially with participants deemed to be vulnerable such as children and people with disabilities. However, as the discussion has shown, the decision to conduct a diary-based study should not be taken lightly, as it requires resourcing and poses a wide range of ethical and methodological dilemmas. Not least of these is balancing the needs and preferences of the participant with those of the research study and researcher. Last of all, it is important to note that there is a 'stark silence' by researchers around ethical issues and the use of social media (Henderson, Johnson, & Auld, 2013). Thus, all of the dilemmas and challenges discussed in this chapter are likely to become increasingly complex, as electronic forms of communication evolve and digital technologies become more advanced.

6 Methodological issues and future directions

In this final chapter, we consider the implications of issues arising in previous chapters for the future of diary methods. We begin by synthesizing conclusions drawn by other researchers who have used this approach and identify strength, limitations and strategies for addressing those limitations, as well as recommendations for good practice in the application of diary methods based on the key principles of inclusive research design and practice.

We then go onto discuss how modern transitions in academic practices, including the growing importance of co-production, mean that diary method can be designed and used in collaborative ways with research participants. Finally, we reflect on the ways in which digital technologies and social media, such as blogging, are creating new possibilities for this method.

Summarizing the strengths and limitations of diary techniques

In reflecting on the case studies, research papers and book chapters that we have drawn on in writing this text, we have been struck by how heavily biased these studies are towards health-related topics – from nutrition to disability, sexual activity, sleep patterns and psychological stressors. Of course this is not the sum total of diary work – indeed the book draws on other examples throughout, but nevertheless, it *does* raise the question of why social scientists have been slower to engage with solicited diary methods that perhaps can be said of those working in the health field. Is it because there remains a dominant perception that solicited diaries are largely quantitative and used to count the number of times an event occurs over a predefined period of time? Is it because social researchers perceive the effort required in undertaking solicited diary techniques may be disproportionate to the value of the data gathered? Is it because there is a misperception that diary techniques are exclusionary to certain groups of people? Or, is it because social researchers have yet to realize the innovative potential that new technologies – from audiovisual to web-based – can offer researchers desiring to use solicited diary techniques? It may even be because diary-based research is actually a complex methodology, particularly when it involves technologies, which requires the researcher to have advanced skills and knowledge in the practice of data collection and analysis. Whatever the case, our aim in this text has been to open up to the reader the wide range of possibilities and benefits that solicited diaries can bring to the social researcher's methodological toolbox. Indeed, other disciplines and fields of research could learn much from how health researchers are using diary techniques and the wide range of participants they are engaging with – including those groups of people often defined as 'vulnerable' – such as young children, victims of sexual abuse, people with dementia and other disabilities.

As we have illustrated throughout the text, solicited diary methods offer far more scope for creativity and methodological complexity than, for example, the structured survey or the semi- or unstructured interview commonly used in social research. The ability to capture events as they happen, using a wide range of paper-based, electronic and web-based approaches, enables a much deeper, insightful and accurate understanding of how specific aspects of a person's life, their experiences of issues or events unfold and change over time. Furthermore, unlike question and response techniques, diaries suffer far less from those problems of recall bias that, some have argued, call into question the internal validity of studies using self-reported data. As noted in Chapter 4, the growing use of portable technology in diary research offers even further potential to reduce any recall bias by enabling participants to record diary data in real time. Moreover, as society become more 'mobile and 24/7 orientated', it is important that researchers develop and use methods (like email diaries) that reflect the day-to-day experiences of its participants (Jones & Woolley, 2014, p. 1).

The examples and case studies on which we have drawn have demonstrated how solicited diary methods can be used as a stand-alone methodological technique using purely written, audio or visual diaries or any combination of these approaches to diary keeping. The rise of audio and visual diary keeping in particular has been important in addressing critiques that diary approaches favour educated middle-class participants and thus are likely to exclude large sections of the population. The visual can also offer unique insights about the body and bodily behaviour 'in the telling'. The many examples we have drawn on in this book reveal the wide range of people from different age groups, cultures and dis/abilities who have participated successfully in diary studies. In particular, the studies we have drawn upon illustrate how participants' choices about what to reveal and what not to reveal in their solicited diaries capture the weight and meaning they attach to particular experiences and events in their lives that is often by-passed in more question and response techniques. Where accuracy and time are methodologically important, they can also capture a level of detail that is often forgotten in more retrospective accounts.

As we have demonstrated throughout the book, solicited diaries can be used in a spectrum of research designs from the very simple (structured diary responses given over a short but intensive period of time) to the more detailed semi- and unstructured diary using a mix of written and/or audio or visual techniques to highly complex multi-method studies using a range of techniques of which the solicited diary may be just one element.

For us, the 'added value' of solicited diaries, whether used as a stand-alone technique or part of a mixed methods study, lies in the time context that underpins it. Not only are data gathered in real time (or as near real time as possible), but by doing so over a defined period of time, it facilitates the unfolding of a longitudinal story, related to the topic of interest, that is framed within the participants' own words or pictures. This time component is one that is wholly absent from the one-off survey, interview or focus group techniques. Even where repeat interviews or surveys are undertaken, they are not gathered at the point of occurrence of the event of interest. Neither do they afford the participant the freedom and control to record the event as and when it makes temporal sense to do so. The solicited diary, however, offers the opportunity to reveal within-person changes over time and a greater reporting of unseen behaviours and settings. It is certainly true that observational or ethnographic techniques are a useful way of uncovering otherwise unseen behaviours, but most contemporary ethnographies (or mini-ethnographies as they are sometimes referred to) no longer engage in those deeply immersive anthropological studies of the past. For the most part, they comprise a series of audiovisual observations of the relational engagement between people and particular environments, settings or events carried out over relatively short, but purposively selected, time frames over a defined period of time. Here, then, the use of solicited diaries *alongside* ethnographic research could considerably strengthen our understanding of important but potentially unseen events that occur when the ethnographer is not 'in the field'.

But the strength of the time context within solicited diary method also relates to the opportunities it offers research participants to think through and record their diary response at their own pace – to structure and restructure their responses should they so desire, until they feel that the response they have given is an accurate reflection of what they actually wanted to say. It is this aspect of solicited diary method, we maintain, that makes it a more empowering technique for research participants. Furthermore, as we have demonstrated, the emergence of new approaches to diary keeping that take the solicited diary technique beyond the traditional paper and ink approach has proven inclusive of a wide range of individuals – overcoming critiques that diary method is exclusive of those whose physical, cognitive or educational attainments prohibit their involvement. It should also be pointed out that people are likely to improve their ability to capture data as time goes on; indeed, we highlighted in Chapter 3 how some studies have involved people in keeping a diary for a year or more. Thus, diary keeping allows for a slower-paced, longitudinal type of research, which may better suit some participants, topic areas and/or settings.

Of course, we cannot ignore the 'messiness' of doing diary research nor the complexities involved in using this method – this temporal unfolding of data within diary techniques presents challenges for analysis. Not only does diary data generate significant amounts of data that need to be sensitively handled, but, as discussed in Chapter 3, to truly gain from these temporal insights we need to avoid falling into the trap of resorting to traditional modes of analysis – whether quantitative or qualitative – in order to ensure that this temporality is not lost. Within quantitative approaches, this may require the researcher to use multilevel modelling techniques and examine the data for lagged effects. Qualitative approaches also need to adopt techniques for analysis that ensure the time context is not lost, for example, by engaging with narrative modes of analysis over thematic or content analysis. In other words, we need to ensure that in seeking to understand key elements of a particular 'scene', we do not lose our understanding of the overall 'plot'.

Addressing limitations

In thinking about the complexities of diary research, we have to recognize that while this approach has many strengths, it also requires considerable effort on the part of both the participant and the researcher if good completion rates are to be assured. We have touched on this in earlier chapters but we cannot reinforce enough the importance of ensuring participants are fully apprised of what is involved at the outset and ensuring appropriate support mechanisms are in place. Regular contact between the researcher and researched can be critical in maintaining participant motivation, alleviating possible respondent fatigue and encouraging continued diary submission where a participant may have stopped returning diary data for any one of a myriad of reasons. In other words, the more effort put into the development and ongoing process of conducting diaries as whole or part of a research study, the greater value you will gain from the data.

Despite our enthusiasm for diary method we need to point out that just like any other approach, it has both strengths and weaknesses. We have set these out for the reader in order to enable him or her to make an informed decision about when, where and with whom the solicited diary might most usefully contribute to the methodological design of a research study and the form it might take. We have summarized these strengths and limitations below, but at the same time, we have set out some strategies to mitigate these limitations. We make no claim that the contents of Table 6.1 are all-encompassing and conclusive – indeed we have every hope that as new approaches to this method develop over time, researchers will update, refine and add to this as a means of providing those researchers who may be newer to this technique with a useful and easily accessible schematic to help inform their methodological decision-making.

Table 6.1 Diary techniques – Summary of strengths and limitations

Strengths	Limitations	Strategies to mitigate limitations
• Provides information recorded at point of action or soon after that may be forgotten in an interview or other responsive mode methods. So reduces recall bias	• Can demand considerable effort both physically and cognitively from participants	• Inform participants of demands at the start; make reasonable adjustments to diary-keeping procedures to enable participation
• Ability to verify date and time of entry using technologies increases quality and confidence of data	• Requires different levels of technical competence of researcher and participant to programme and use equipment	• Build in time and resources for training researchers/ participant in use of equipment and checking
• Involves the users in an active manner. Provides deeper understanding of the activities the users engage in	• As with surveys, structured diaries can be difficult to interpret due to lack of context information	• Consider building in time for follow-up diary interviews
• Is useful for obtaining real-life measures/ accounts of the activities and experiences of participants	• Can generate significant amounts of data taking time to analyse	• Provide participants with an upper and lower limit for audio-diary entries and photograph; select relevant data for analysis; accept that some date will be unusable
• Useful for collecting sensitive information that may be less readily gained using face-to-face research techniques	• Relies on the informant's ability and motivation to complete diary	• Provide financial incentives; remind people of the importance and value of the data they are collecting
• Can be used to supplement other research techniques with a rich source of information on respondents' behaviour and experiences on a daily basis	• Where recording is required over a period of time, study fatigue may set in resulting in poorer quality recording towards end of study	• Offer support to participants while they are diary keeping; consider using electronic diary
• Relatively low cost to administer	• Attrition and gaps in entries may be an issue	• Set a realistic diary-keeping time frame; consider including gaps in data collection; consider electronic diaries where reminders can be set
• Flexibility: can be used to collect numerical or textual data or a combination of both	• Diary-keeping equipment may add costs	• Take the cost of equipment into account when deciding on the form of diary keeping; ask participants to use own equipment (e.g. smartphone) if appropriate

Solicited diaries: Co-production and inclusive research

The Research Councils UK Public Engagement with Research Strategy (2014) notes that:

> Relevance, trust, accountability and transparency are the cornerstones of the relationship between research and society. It is vital that the public have access to the knowledge research generates and the opportunity to influence the questions that research is seeking to address (Research Council, 2014).

This changing landscape of research has arguably been led once again by a health research framework developed in the mid-1990s and concerned to increase the impact and relevance of health research through embedding public and patient involvement in research and a more general shift towards co-production (see NIHR INVOLVE, http://www.invo.org.uk/about-involve/). Recognition of the value of this approach is evident through its increased adoption in other spheres and fields of social and applied research. As we have discussed in Chapter 5, this involves research *with* rather than *on* people – well-designed semi- or unstructured solicited diary studies provide participants with the opportunity to shape both the pace and nature of diary data collection. It enables them to give voice to those thoughts, experiences and actions that are meaningful to them, giving them choice and control over what they choose to reveal and how they reveal it. Recording the data in the absence of the researcher facilitates a sense of non-judgementalism and addresses those traditional imbalances of power that often exist between the researcher and researched. This approach to the application of diary methods offers opportunities for good research practice based on the key principles of inclusive research design and practice.

The pedagogical landscape

While the diary method has much to recommend it, from our experiences, it does not tend to be privileged or taught as part of the panoply of approaches to research methods at undergraduate, graduate or doctoral level. Pedagogically, research methods teaching tends to privilege either the interview or focus group approach in qualitative methods teaching (with occasional forays into ethnography and documentary analysis) or the survey and/or randomized control trial approaches within quantitative techniques. As even a cursory investigation of research methods courses advertised online reveals, rarely does diary method feature on the syllabus. Yet its potential for time-sequenced investigation using a vast range of techniques from the documentary and linguistic, to the visual, thematic, statistical and multilevelled analysis makes it a valuable research tool – one that, as already demonstrated, addresses critiques of recall bias often directed at more commonly taught research methods. At the very least, those designing research methods courses would do well to rethink their methodological priorities and introduce students to the possibilities of solicited diary techniques. Indeed, we would argue that pedagogically, diary methods should not be viewed as an uncommon technique with limited utility, rather they need to be seen as a methodological tool that is equally, if not more, valid than those more commonly taught techniques.

Future directions

In this section, we discuss some future directions for those interested in engaging with diary research. As discussed throughout the text, a growing number of researchers are beginning to recognize the potential added value of solicited diary method in social research – whether as a stand-alone method or as an approach in part of a multi-method study. We foresee that this will continue to grow in strength and that, of itself, will trigger further innovative developments. However, it is perhaps the rise of digital technologies and their integration into research methods that holds the most promise. These developments mean that researchers will increasingly find themselves having to engage with, and adapt to, the digital culture. The growth of ubiquitous technologies, smartphones, tablets and so forth means that we are shifting towards a scenario in which the research equipment required for undertaking solicited diary research may be significantly simplified. The capability is now there for research to be undertaken through one device that has multiple capacities and features to facilitate video, audio and electronic-written diary keeping. Such devices will become an increasingly common part of daily life within many households, particularly in high-income countries. While currently technological advance still raises issues of access for older people who are less conversant or comfortable using these new technologies, the next generation of older people – for example, the baby boomers and those following in their wake – will be increasingly comfortable with these new technologies opening up new opportunities for how solicited diaries can be developed and the multiple forms diary data can take. We should not forget, however, that access to, and familiarity with, digital technologies can still raise issues of access for those who are less affluent (including those living in less developed parts of the world) and those whose physical, sensory or cognitive limitations may require specially adapted equipment. Yet even in developing countries, access to the internet is becoming a growing necessity in the information and digital age that we live in – although clearly who has access to this will vary significantly. For some people, more traditional audio or 'paper and pen' based diaries will continue to remain the most accessible approach – but even here, software advances in voice recognition may facilitate the ability of those with visual or physical impairments to participate.

In recognizing how technology is opening up new opportunities and new forms of structured diary research, we also need to recognize how technology is changing the nature of our society. The growth of self-disclosure practices through blogging, social media such as Facebook and Twitter, the rise of the 'selfie' is re-energizing the practice of diary keeping but in much more public and interactive ways than we have seen in the past. Weblogs, for example, are simultaneously public and personal diaries. They are intended to be read and to provoke dialogue with others. This presents opportunities for researchers to solicit online diaries or to analyse existing online diary data in ways that have not previously been possible. Arguably, then, the boundaries between solicited and unsolicited diaries are blurring due to web-based applications and practices such as blogging and Facebook, presenting researchers with challenges to the traditional notions of solicited and unsolicited diaries.

Final remarks

Clearly, the internet and digital technologies are opening up a whole new avenue of potential for the solicited diary method. However, while the possibilities are endless, these developments will inevitably raise tensions and dilemmas – not least the ethical dilemmas of how to distinguish between the public and private in new online forms of diary keeping, the boundary between solicited and unsolicited diary data and who (if anyone) may find themselves excluded from these new technological approaches to diary research. Given the pace of change, however, the challenge will not simply be one of ethics and how to incorporate technology into the design and application of solicited diary research, but one of keeping up with these rapidly shifting technologies themselves. Hence, while technology offers exciting new opportunities, it is highly likely that paper-based approaches will still have a place for the foreseeable future.

Notes

Chapter 2

1   For more detailed information and examples of how structured diaries are used in time-use social science research, visit the Time Use Centre website http://www.timeuse.org/.

2   For a detailed discussion of sensory methodologies, see Pink (2007, 2009).

Chapter 3

1   See Eynden, Corti, Bishop, and Horton (2011) for a general discussion about good practice in the sharing and management of research data.

References

Alaszewski, A. (2006a). *Using diaries for social research*. London: Sage Publications.

Alaszewski, A. (2006b). Diaries as a source of suffering narratives: A critical commentary. *Health, Risk & Society*, 8(1), 43–58. doi:10.1080/13698570500532553

Aldridge, J. (2007). Picture this: The use of participatory photographic research methods with people with learning disabilities. *Disability & Society*, 22(1), 1–17. doi:10.1080/09687590601056006

Alfvén, G. (2010). SMS pain diary: A method for real-time data capture of recurrent pain in childhood. *Acta Paediatrica (Oslo, Norway: 1992)*, 99(7), 1047–1053. doi:10.1111/j.1651-2227.2010.01735.x

Allen, L. (2009). 'Snapped': Researching the sexual cultures of schools using visual methods. *International Journal of Qualitative Studies in Education*, 22(5), 549–561. doi:10.1080/09518390903051523

Anastario, M., & Schmalzbauer, L. (2008). Piloting the time diary method among Honduran immigrants: Gendered time use. *Journal of Immigrant and Minority Health/Center for Minority Public Health*, 10(5), 437–443. doi:10.1007/s10903-007-9109-z

Atkinson, P., & Silverman, D. (1997). Kundera's immortality: The interview society and the invention of the self. *Qualitative Inquiry*, 3(3) 304–325.

Axhausen, K. W., Löchl, M., Schlich, R., Buhl, T., & Widmer, P. (2006). Fatigue in long-duration travel diaries. *Transportation*, 34(2), 143–160. doi:10.1007/s11116-006-9106-4

Bailey, C., Foran, T. G., Ni Scanaill, C., & Dromey, B. (2011). Older adults, falls and technologies for independent living: A life space approach. *Ageing and Society*, 31(5), 829–848. doi:10.1017/S0144686X10001170

Bancroft, A., Karels, M., Meadhbh, Ó., & Jade, M. (2014). Not being there: Research at a distance with video. In M. Hand & S. Hillyard (Eds.), *Big data? Qualitative approaches to digital research* (Vol. 13, pp. 137–153). Bingley: Emerald Group Publishing Ltd. doi:10.1108/S1042-31922014000013009

Barker, M., & Gill, R. (2012). Sexual subjectification and Bitchy Jones's Diary. *Psychology & Sexuality, 3*(1), 26–40. Retrieved from http://www.tandfonline.com/doi/abs/10.1080/19419899.2011.627693

Bartlett, R. (2012). Modifying the diary interview method to research the lives of people with dementia. *Qualitative Health Research, 22*(12), 1717–1726. doi:10.1177/1049732312462240

Bass, B. L., Linney, K. D., Butler, A. B., & Grzywacz, J. G. (2007). Evaluating PDAs for data collection in family research with non-professional couples. *Community, Work & Family, 10*(1), 57–74. doi:10.1080/13668800601110785

Bates, C. (2013). Video diaries: Audio-visual research methods and the elusive body. *Visual Studies, 28*(1), 29–37. doi:10.1080/1472586X.2013.765203

Bedwell, C., McGowan, L., & Lavender, T. (2012). Using diaries to explore midwives' experiences in intrapartum care: An evaluation of the method in a phenomenological study. *Midwifery, 28*(2), 150–155. doi:10.1016/j.midw.2010.12.007

Bellisle, F., Dalix, A., & de Castro, J. M. (1999). Eating patterns in French subjects studied by the 'weekly food diary' method. *Appetite, 32*(1), 46–52. Retrieved from http://www.ncbi.nlm.nih.gov/pubmed/9989913

Bijoux, D., & Myers, J. (2006). Interviews, solicited diaries and photography: 'New' ways of accessing everyday experiences of place. *Graduate Journal of Asia-Pacific Studies, 4*(1), 44–64.

Blinka, L., Subrahmanyam, K., Smahel, D., & Seganti, F. R. (2012). Differences in the teen blogosphere: Insights from a content analysis of English- and Czech-language weblogs. *Young, 20*(3), 277–296. doi:10.1177/110330881202000304

Bogdanovic, D., Dowd, M., Wattam, E., & Adam, A. (2012). Contesting methodologies: Evaluating focus group and privacy diary methods in a study of on-line privacy. *Journal of Information, Communication and Ethics in Society, 10*(4), 208–221. doi:10.1108/14779961211285854

Bolger, N., Davis, A., & Rafaeli, E. (2003). Diary methods: Capturing life as it is lived. *Annual Review of Psychology, 54*, 579–616. doi:10.1146/annurev.psych.54.101601.145030

Bonato, P. (2005). Advances in wearable technology and applications in physical medicine and rehabilitation. *Journal of Neuroengineering and Rehabilitation, 2*(1), 2. doi:10.1186/1743-0003-2-2

Boone, M. R., Cook, S. H., & Wilson, P. (2013). Substance use and sexual risk behavior in HIV-positive men who have sex with men: An episode-level analysis. *AIDS and Behavior, 17*(5), 1883–1887. doi:10.1007/s10461-012-0167-4

Bowling, A. (2014). *Research methods in health: Investigating health and health services* (4th ed.). Maidenhead: Open University Press.

Brennan, N., Corrigan, O., Allard, J., Archer, J., Barnes, R., Bleakley, A., de Bere, S. R. (2010). The transition from medical student to junior doctor: Today's experiences of tomorrow's doctors. *Medical Education, 44*(5), 449–458. doi:10.1111/j.1365-2923.2009.03604.x

Bright, E., Drake, M. J., & Abrams, P. (2011). Urinary diaries : Evidence for the development and validation of diary content, format, and duration. *Neurourology and Urodynamics, 30*(3), 348–352. doi:10.1002/nau

Brown, B., Sellen, A., & O'hara, K. (2000). A diary study of information capture in working life. In *CHI 2005 Papers: Understanding users and usage patterns* (Vol. 2, pp. 438–445). Retrieved from http://dl.acm.org/citation.cfm?id=332472

Brown, K. (2011). 'Vulnerability': Handle with care. *Ethics and Social Welfare, 5*(3), 313–321. doi:10.1080/17496535.2011.597165

Brown, K. (2012). Re-moralising 'Vulnerability'. *People Place and Policy Online, 6*(1), 41–53. doi:10.3351/ppp.0006.0001.0005

Buchwald, D. (2009). Video diary data collection in research with children: An alternative method. *International Journal of Qualitative Methods, 8*(1), 12–20.

Buckingham, D., & Willett, R. (2006). *Digital generations: Children, young people, and new media.* Mahwah, NJ: Lawrence Erlbaum Associates.

Bullingham, L., & Vasconcelos, A. C. (2013). 'The presentation of self in the online world': Goffman and the study of online identities. *Journal of Information Science, 39*(1), 101–112. doi:10.1177/0165551512470051

Bureau, C. H., Services, H., & Science, F. S. (2005). How reliable are fathers' reports of involvement with their children? A methodological report. *Fathering, 3*(1), 81–92.

Burton, C., Weller, D., & Sharpe, M. (2007). Are electronic diaries useful for symptoms research? A systematic review. *Journal of Psychosomatic Research, 62*(5), 553–561. doi:10.1016/j.jpsychores.2006.12.022

Bylsma, L. M., Croon, M. A., Vingerhoets, A. J. J. M., & Rottenberg, J. (2011). When and for whom does crying improve mood? A daily diary study of 1004 crying episodes. *Journal of Research in Personality, 45*(4), 385–392. doi:10.1016/j.jrp.2011.04.007

Cleveland, H. H., & Harris, K. S. (2010). The role of coping in moderating within-day associations between negative triggers and substance use cravings: A daily diary investigation. *Addictive Behaviors, 35*(1), 60–63. doi:10.1016/j.addbeh.2009.08.010

Connelly, M., & Bickel, J. (2011). An electronic daily diary process study of stress and health behavior triggers of primary headaches in children. *Journal of Pediatric Psychology, 36*(8), 852–862. doi:10.1093/jpepsy/jsr017

Corti, L. (1993). Using diaries in social research. Social Research Update 1. Retrieved 14 December 2014 from http://sru.soc.surrey.ac.uk/SRU2.html

Coxon, A. P. (1999). Parallel accounts? Discrepancies between self-report (diary) and recall (questionnaire) measures of the same sexual behaviour. *AIDS Care, 11*(2), 221–234. doi:10.1080/09540129948108

Creswell, J. (2014). *Research design: Qualitative, quantitative, mixed methods approaches* (4th ed.). Thousand Oaks, CA: Sage.

Edinburgh, L. D., Garcia, C. M., & Saewyc, E. M. (2013). It's called 'Going out to play': A video diary study of Hmong girls' perspectives on running away. *Health Care for Women International, 34*(2), 150–168. doi:10.1080/07399332.2011.645962

Elg, M., Witell, L., Poksinska, B., Engström, J., Dahlgaard-Park, S. M., & Kammerlind, P. (2011). Solicited diaries as a means of involving patients in development of healthcare services. *International Journal of Quality and Service Sciences, 3*(2), 128–145. doi:10.1108/17566691111146050

Eynden, A. V. Van Den, Corti, L., Bishop, L., & Horton, L. (2011). *Managing and sharing data.* Retrieved 29 December 2014 from http://www.dataarchive.ac.uk/media/2894/managingsharing.pdf

Feeney, J. A. (2002). Attachment, marital interaction, and relationship satisfaction: A diary study. *Personal Relationships, 9*(1), 39–55. doi:10.1111/1475-6811.00003

Flewitt, R. (2006). Using video to investigate preschool classroom interaction: Education research assumptions and methodological practices. *Visual Communication, 5*(1), 25–50. doi:10.1177/1470357206060917

Flick, U. (2014). *An introduction to qualitative research* (5th ed.). London: Sage.

Fricke, J., & Unsworth, C. (2001). Time use and importance of instrumental activities of daily living. *Australian Occupational Therapy Journal, 48*, 118–131.

Gibson, B. E. (2002). The integrated use of audio diaries, photography, and interviews in research with disabled young men. *International Journal of Qualitative Research Methods, 12,* 382–402.

Gibson, V. (1995). An analysis of the use of diaries as a data collection method. *Nurse Researcher, 3*(1), 61–68.

Graham, C. A, Catania, J. A, Brand, R., Duong, T., & Canchola, J. A. (2003). Recalling sexual behavior: A methodological analysis of memory recall bias via interview using the diary as the gold standard. *Journal of Sex Research, 40*(4), 325–332. doi:10.1080/00224490209552198

Green, A. S., Rafaeli, E., Bolger, N., Shrout, P. E., & Reis, H. T. (2006). Paper or plastic? Data equivalence in paper and electronic diaries. *Psychological Methods, 11*(1), 87–105. doi:10.1037/1082-989X.11.1.87

Gregory, R., Walwyn, L., Bloor, S., & Amin, S. (2006). A feasibility study of the use of photographic food diaries in the management of obesity. *Practical Diabetes International, 23*(2), 66–68.

Gershuny, J. (2000). *Changing times: Work and lesiure in postindustrial society.* Oxford: Oxford University Press.

Hammersley, M. (2013). *What is qualitative research?* London: Bloomsbury Publishing.

Hardy, S., & Gray, R. (2012). The secret food diary of a person diagnosed with schizophrenia. *Journal of Psychiatric and Mental Health Nursing, 19*(7), 603–609. doi:10.1111/j.1365-2850.2011.01826.x

Hawkes, G., Houghton, J., & Rowe, G. (2009). Risk and worry in everyday life: Comparing diaries and interviews as tools in risk perception research. *Health, Risk & Society, 11*(3), 209–230. doi:10.1080/13698570902906439

Hellström, I., Nolan, M., Nordenfelt, L., & Lundh, U. (2007). Ethical and methodological issues in interviewing persons with dementia. *Nursing Ethics, 14*(5), 608–619. doi:10.1177/0969733007080206

Henderson, M., Johnson, N. F., & Auld, G. (2013). Silences of ethical practice: Dilemmas for researchers using social media. *Educational Research and Evaluation, 19*(6), 546–560. doi:10.1080/13803 611.2013.805656

Herbenick, D., Hensel, D., Smith, N. K., Schick, V., Reece, M., Sanders, S. A., & Fortenberry, J. D. (2013). Pubic hair removal and sexual behavior: Findings from a prospective daily diary study of sexually active women in the United States. *The Journal of Sexual Medicine, 10*(3), 678–685. doi:10.1111/jsm.12031

Hislop, J., Arber, S., Meadows, R., & Venn, S. (2005). Narratives of the night: The use of audio diaries researching sleep. *Sociological Research Online, 10*(4).

Hookway, N. (2008). 'Entering the blogosphere': Some strategies for using blogs in social research. *Qualitative Research, 8*(1), 91–113. doi:10.1177/1468794107085298

Hooley, T., Marriott, J., & Wellens, J. (2013). *What is online research*. New York: Bloomsbury Academic Publishing.

Howland, M., & Rafaeli, E. (2010). Bringing everyday mind reading into everyday life: Assessing empathic accuracy with daily diary data. *Journal of Personality, 78*(5), 1437–1468. doi:10.1111/j.1467-6494.2010.00657.x

Informa, R., Number, W. R., House, M., Street, M., Writing, D., Interpretative, A., & Journal, A. I. (2010). Diary writing : An interpretative research method of teaching and learning. *Educational Research and Evaluation, 8*(2), 149–168.

Jacelon, C. S., & Imperio, K. (2005). Participant diaries as a source of data in research with older adults. *Qualitative Health Research, 15*(7), 991–997. doi:10.1177/1049732305278603

Jackson, S., & Vares, T. (2013). 'Perfect skin', 'pretty skinny': Girls' embodied identities and post-feminist popular culture. *Journal of Gender Studies*, March 2014, 1–14. doi:10.1080/09589236.2013.841573

Jahoda, M., Lazarsfeld, P., & Zeisel, H. (1972). *Marienthal: The sociology of an unemployed community*. London: Tavistock Publications.

Jent, J. F., Eaton, C. K., Merrick, M. T., Englebert, N. E., Dandes, S. K., Chapman, A. V., & Hershorin, E. R. (2011). The decision to access patient information from a social media site: What would you do? *The Journal of Adolescent Health : Official Publication of the Society for Adolescent Medicine, 49*(4), 414–420. doi:10.1016/j.jadohealth.2011.02.004

Johnson, J., & Bytheway, B. (2001). An evaluation of the use of diaries in a study of medication in later life. *International Journal of Social Research Methodology, 4*(3), 183–204. doi:10.1080/13645570010029467

Jones, A., & Wooley, J. (2014) The email diary: A promising tool for the twenty-first century? *Qualitative Research*. Published online before print, 31 December 2014. doi:10.1177/1468794114561347

Jones, P. (2012). Sensory indiscipline and affect: A study of commuter cycling. *Social & Cultural Geography, 13*(6), 645–658. doi:10.1080/146493 65.2012.713505

Katz, I. R., Morales, K., Datto, C., Streim, J., Oslin, D., DiFilippo, S., & Have, T. T. (2005). Probing for affective side effects of drugs used in geriatric practice: Use of daily diaries to test for effects of metoclopramide and naproxen. *Neuropsychopharmacology : Official Publication of the American College of Neuropsychopharmacology, 30*(8), 1568–1575. doi:10.1038/sj.npp.1300751

Keleher, H. M., & Verrinder, G. K. (2003). Health diaries in a rural Australian study. *Qualitative Health Research, 13*(3), 435–443. doi:10.1177/1049732302250342

Kempke, S., Luyten, P., Claes, S., Van Wambeke, P., Bekaert, P., Goossens, L., & Van Houdenhove, B. (2013). The prevalence and impact of early childhood trauma in Chronic Fatigue Syndrome. *Journal of Psychiatric Research, 47*(5), 664–669. doi:10.1016/j.jpsychires.2013.01.021

Kim, Y. M., Rieh, S. Y., Yang, J. Y., & St Jean, B. (2009). An online activity diary method for studying credibility assessment on the Web. Proceedings of the American Society for Information Science and Technology, 46(1), 1–5.

Koopman-Boyden, P., & Richardson, M. (2013). An evaluation of mixed methods (diaries and focus groups) when working with older people. *International Journal of Social Research Methodology, 16*(5), 389–401. doi:10.1080/13645579.2012.716971

Kristo, G., Janssen, S. M. J., & Murre, J. M. J. (2009). Retention of autobiographical memories: An Internet-based diary study. *Memory (Hove, England), 17*(8), 816–829. doi:10.1080/09658210903143841

Lämsä, T., Rönkä, A., Poikonen, P.-L., & Malinen, K. (2012). The child diary as a research tool. *Early Child Development and Care, 182*(3–4), 469–486. doi:10.1080/03004430.2011.646725

Lanigan, J. A., Wells, J. C., Lawson, M. S., & Lucas, A. (2001). Validation of food diary method for assessment of dietary energy and macronutrient intake in infants and children aged 6-24 months. *European Journal of Clinical Nutrition, 55* (2), 124–129. Retrieved from http://www.ncbi.nlm.nih.gov/pubmed/11305625

Latham, A. (2003). Research, performance, and doing human geography: Some reflections on the diary-photograph, diary-interview method. *Environment and Planning A, 35*(11), 1993–2017. doi:10.1068/a3587

Laurenceau, J.-P., & Bolger, N. (2005). Using diary methods to study marital and family processes. *Journal of Family Psychology : JFP : Journal of the Division of Family Psychology of the American Psychological Association (Division 43), 19*(1), 86–97. doi:10.1037/0893-3200.19.1.86

Lawson, A., Robinson, I., & Bakes, C. (1985). Problems in evaluating the consequences of disabling illness: The case of multiple sclerosis. *Psychological Medicine, 15*(3), 555–579. Retrieved from http://www.ncbi.nlm.nih.gov/pubmed/4048316

Lee, Y. J., & Gretzel, U. (2014). Cross-cultural differences in social identity formation through travel blogging. *Journal of Travel & Tourism Marketing, 31*(1), 37–54. doi:10.1080/10548408.2014.861701

Lehavot, K., Ben-Zeev, D., & Neville, R. E. (2012). Ethical considerations and social media: A case of suicidal postings on Facebook. *Journal of Dual Diagnosis, 8*(4), 341–346. doi:10.1080/15504263.2012.718928

Lillegaard, I. T. L., Løken, E. B., & Andersen, L. F. (2007). Relative validation of a pre-coded food diary among children, under-reporting varies with reporting day and time of the day. *European Journal of Clinical Nutrition, 61*(1), 61–68. doi:10.1038/sj.ejcn.1602487

Lundqvist, C., Rugland, E., Clench-Aas, J., Bartonova, A., & Hofoss, D. (2010). Children are reliable reporters of common symptoms: Results from a self-reported symptom diary for primary school children. *Acta Paediatrica (Oslo, Norway: 1992), 99*(7), 1054–1059. doi:10.1111/j.1651-2227.2010.01727.x

Meth, P. (2003). Entries and omissions: Using solicited diaries in geographical research. *Area, 35*(2), 195–205.

Milligan, C., Bingley, A., & Gatrell, A. (2005). Digging deep: Using diary techniques to explore the place of health and well-being amongst older people. *Social Science & Medicine (1982), 61*(9), 1882–1892. doi:10.1016/j.socscimed.2005.04.002

Minnis, A. M., & Padian, N. S. (2001). Reliability of adolescents' self-reported sexual behavior: A comparison of two diary methodologies. *The Journal of Adolescent Health : Official Publication of the Society for Adolescent Medicine, 28*(5), 394–403. Retrieved from http://www.ncbi.nlm.nih.gov/pubmed/11336869

Mizen, P. (2005). A little 'light work'? Children's images of their labour. *Visual Studies, 20*(2), 124–139. doi:10.1080/14725860500244001

Moloney, M. F., Aycock, D. M., Cotsonis, G. A., Myerburg, S., Farino, C., & Lentz, M. (2009). An internet-based migraine headache diary: Issues in internet-based research. *Headache: The Journal of Head and Face Pain, 49*(5), 673–686. doi:10.1111/j.1526-4610.2009.01399.x

Monrouxe, L. V. (2009). Solicited audio diaries in longitudinal narrative research: A view from inside. *Qualitative Research, 9*(1), 81–103. doi:10.1177/1468794108098032

Moore, T. M., Elkins, S. R., McNulty, J. K., Kivisto, A. J., & Handsel, V. A. (2011). Alcohol use and intimate partner violence perpetration among college students: Assessing the temporal association using electronic diary technology. *Psychology of Violence, 1*(4), 315–328. doi:10.1037/a0025077

Morrison, C.-A. (2012). Heterosexuality and home: Intimacies of space and spaces of touch. *Emotion, Space and Society, 5*(1), 10–18. doi:10.1016/j.emospa.2010.09.001

Mort, M., Convery, I., Baxter, J., & Bailey, C. (2005). Psychosocial effects of the 2001 UK foot and mouth disease epidemic in a rural population: Qualitative diary based study. *BMJ (Clinical Research Ed.), 331*(7527), 1234. doi:10.1136/bmj.38603.375856.68

Nässla, H., & Carr, D. A. (2003). Investigating intra-family communication using photo diaries. *Proceedings HCI International, 2*, 22–27.

Nes, A. A. G., Eide, H., Kristjánsdóttir, Ó. B., & van Dulmen, S. (2013). Web-based, self-management enhancing interventions with e-diaries and personalized feedback for persons with chronic illness: A tale of three studies. *Patient Education and Counseling, 93*(3), 451–458. doi:10.1016/j.pec.2013.01.022

Nicholl, H. (2010). Diaries as a method of data collection in research. *Paediatric Nursing, 22*(7), 16–20. doi:10.7748/paed2010.09.22.7.16.c7948

Noyes, A. (2004). Video diary: A method for exploring learning dispositions. *Cambridge Journal of Education, 34*(2), 193–209. doi:10.1080/0305764041000170561

Noyes, A. (2009). Using video diaries to investigate learner trajectories: Researching the unknown knowns. In P. Thomson (Ed.), *Doing visual research with children and young people*. New York: Routledge.

O'Donnell, S. C., Marshman, Z., & Zaitoun, H. (2013). 'Surviving the sting': The use of solicited diaries in children and young people with oral mucosal disease. *International Journal of Paediatric Dentistry/the British Paedodontic Society [and] the International Association of Dentistry for Children, 23*(5), 352–358. doi:10.1111/ipd.12028

Okami, P. (2002). Dear diary: A useful but imperfect method. In M. Wiederman & B. E. Whitley (Eds.), *Handbook for conducting research on human sexuality*. Mahwah, NJ: Lawrence Erlbaum Associates Publishers.

Olive, R. (2012). 'Making friends with the neighbours': Blogging as a research method. *International Journal of Cultural Studies, 16*(1), 71–84. doi:10.1177/1367877912441438

Orban, K., Edberg, A.-K., & Erlandsson, L.-K. (2012). Using a time-geographical diary method in order to facilitate reflections on changes in patterns of daily occupations. *Scandinavian Journal of Occupational Therapy, 19*(3), 249–259. doi:10.3109/11038128.2011.620981

Palen, L., Salzman, M., & Street, W. T. (2002). Voice-mail diary studies for naturalistic data capture under mobile conditions. Retrieved 29 December 2014 from https://www.cs.colorado.edu/~palen/palen_papers/palen-diarystudy.pdf

Papp, L. M., Goeke-Morey, M. C., & Cummings, E. M. (2007). Linkages between spouses' psychological distress and marital conflict in the home. *Journal of Family Psychology : JFP : Journal of the Division of Family Psychology of the American Psychological Association (Division 43), 21*(3), 533–537. doi:10.1037/0893-3200.21.3.533

Parker, C., & Pfeiffer, S. (2005). Video blogging: Content to the max. *MultiMedia, IEEE*, 4–8. Retrieved from http://ieeexplore.ieee.org/xpls/abs_all.jsp?arnumber=1423925

Piasecki, T., & Hufford, M. (2007). Assessing clients in their natural environments with electronic diaries: Rationale, benefits, limitations, and barriers. *Psychological ..., 19*(1), 25–43. doi:10.1037/1040-3590.19.1.25

Pickering, D., Horrocks, L. M., Visser, K. S., & Todd, G. (2013). 'Every picture tells a story': Interviews and diaries with children with cerebral palsy about adapted cycling. *Journal of Paediatrics and Child Health, 49*(12), 1040–1044. doi:10.1111/jpc.12289

Pink, S. (2007). *Doing visual ethnography*. London: Sage.

Pink, S. (2009). *Doing sensory ethnography*. London: Sage.

Plowman, L., & Stevenson, O. (2012). Using mobile phone diaries to explore children's everyday lives. *Childhood, 19*(4), 539–553. doi:10.1177/0907568212440014

Power, A and Bartlett, R. (2015). Self-building safe havens in a post-service landscape: how adults with learning disabilities are reclaiming the welcoming communities agenda. *Social & Cultural Geography*.

Powers, A. C. (2008). Social networking as ethical discourse: Blogging a practical and normative library ethic. *Journal of Library Administration, 47*(3–4), 191–209. doi:10.1080/01930820802186522

Prosser, J., & Schwartz, D. (1998). Photographs within the sociological research process. In J. Prosser (Ed.), *Image based research: A qualitative sourcebook for researchers*. London: Falmer Press.

Punch, S. (2002). Research with children: The same or different from research with adults? *Childhood, 9*(3), 321–341. doi:10.1177/0907568202009003005

Reeves, P. (1913). *Round about a pound a week*. London: Bell & Sons.

Research Council (2014). *RCUK Public Engagement with Research Strategy*. Retrieved 29 December 2014 from http://www.rcuk.ac.uk/pe/public-engagement-with-research-strategy/

Rich, M., & Patashnick, J. (2002). Narrative research with audiovisual data: Video intervention/prevention assessment (VIA) and NVivo. *International Journal of Social Research Methodology, 5*(3), 245–261. doi:10.1080/13645570210166373

Richardson, A. (1994). The health diary: An examination of its use as a data collection method. *Journal of Advanced Nursing, 19*(4), 782–791.

Roberts, J. (2011). Video diaries: A tool to investigate sustainability-related learning in threshold spaces. *Environmental Education Research, 17*(5), 675–688. doi:10.1080/13504622.2011.572160

Rönkä, A., Malinen, K., Kinnunen, U., Tolvanen, A., & Lämsä, T. (2010). Capturing daily family dynamics via text messages: Development of the mobile diary. *Community, Work & Family, 13*(1), 5–21. doi:10.1080/13668800902823581

Rook, K. S. (2010). Emotional health and positive versus negative social exchanges : A daily diary analysis. *Applied Developmental Science, 5*(2), 37–41. doi:10.1207/S1532480XADS0502

Ryan, E. B. (2006). Writing through health adversity. *Journal of Language and Social Psychology, 25*(4), 423–436.

Seltzer, M. M., Greenberg, J. S., Hong, J., Smith, L. E., Almeida, D. M., Coe, C., & Stawski, R. S. (2010). Maternal cortisol levels and behavior problems in adolescents and adults with ASD. *Journal of Autism and Developmental Disorders, 40*(4), 457–469. doi:10.1007/s10803-009-0887-0

Sheridan, D. (1993). Writing to the archive: Mass observation as writing auto/biography. *Sociology, 2*(1), 27–40.

Small, L., Sidora-Arcoleo, K., Vaughan, L., Creed-Capsel, J., Chung, K.-Y., & Stevens, C. (2009). Validity and Reliability of Photographic Diet Diaries for Assessing Dietary Intake Among Young Children. *ICAN: Infant, Child, & Adolescent Nutrition, 1*(1), 27–36. doi:10.1177/1941406408330360

Stephens, M. A. P., Franks, M. M., Rook, K. S., Iida, M., Hemphill, R. C., & Salem, J. K. (2013). Spouses' attempts to regulate day-to-day dietary adherence among patients with type 2 diabetes. *Health Psychology : Official Journal of the Division of Health Psychology, American Psychological Association, 32*(10), 1029–1037. doi:10.1037/a0030018

Stone, E., & Priestley, M. (1996). Parasites, pawns and partners: Disability research and the role of non-disabled researchers. *British Journal of Sociology, 47*(4), 109–210.

Tamminen, K. A., & Holt, N. L. (2010). Female adolescent athletes' coping: A season-long investigation. *Journal of Sports Sciences, 28*(1), 101–114. doi:10.1080/02640410903406182

Tennen, H., Affleck, G., Coyne, J. C., Larsen, R. J., & Delongis, A. (2006). Paper and plastic in daily diary research: Comment on Green, Rafaeli, Bolger, Shrout, and Reis (2006). *Psychological Methods, 11*(1), 112–118; discussion 123–5. doi:10.1037/1082-989X.11.1.112

Thomas, F. (2006). Stigma, fatigue and social breakdown: Exploring the impacts of HIV/AIDS on patient and carer well-being in the Caprivi Region, Namibia. *Social Science & Medicine (1982), 63*(12), 3174–3187. doi:10.1016/j.socscimed.2006.08.016

Thomas, F. (2007). Eliciting emotions in HIV/AIDS research: A diary-based approach. *Area, 39*(1), 74–82. doi:10.1111/j.1475-4762.2007.00723.x

Thorne, S. (2011). Toward methodological emancipation in applied health research. *Qualitative Health Research, 21*(4), 443–453. doi: 10.1177/1049732310392595

Tishler, C. L., & Bartholomae, S. (2002). The recruitment of normal healthy volunteers : A review of the literature. *Journal of Clinical Pharmacology, 42*(4), 365–375.

Tov, W., Ng, K. L., Lin, H., & Qiu, L. (2013). Detecting well-being via computerized content analysis of brief diary entries. *Psychological Assessment, 25*(4), 1069–1078. doi:10.1037/a0033007

Ulrich, C., & Grady, C. (2004). Financial incentives and response rates in nursing research. *Nursing Research, 53*(2), 73–74.

Ulrich, L. (1991). *A midwives tale: The Life of Martha Ballard based on her diaries (1785–1812)*. New York: Random House Publishers, Vintage Books.

Välimäki, T., Vehviläinen-Julkunen, K., & Pietilä, A.-M. (2007). Diaries as research data in a study on family caregivers of people with Alzheimer's disease: Methodological issues. *Journal of Advanced Nursing, 59*(1), 68–76. doi:10.1111/j.1365-2648.2007.04273.x

Vansteelandt, K., Rijmen, F., Pieters, G., Probst, M., & Vanderlinden, J. (2007). Drive for thinness, affect regulation and physical activity in eating disorders: A daily life study. *Behaviour Research and Therapy, 45*(8), 1717–1734. doi:10.1016/j.brat.2006.12.005

Venn, S., Arber, S., Meadows, R., & Hislop, J. (2008). The fourth shift: Exploring the gendered nature of sleep disruption among couples with children. *The British Journal of Sociology, 59*(1), 79–97. doi:10.1111/j.1468-4446.2007.00183.x

Voorveld, H. A. M., & van der Goot, M. (2013). Age differences in media multitasking: A diary study. *Journal of Broadcasting & Electronic Media, 57*(3), 392–408. doi:10.1080/08838151.2013.816709

Waldron, I., & Eyer, J. (1975). Socioeconomic causes of the recent rise in death rates for 15-24 year olds. *Social Science & Medicine, 9*(7), 383–396.

Walshe, N. (2013). Exploring and developing children's understandings of sustainable development with dialogic diaries. *Children's Geographies, 11*(1), 132–154. doi:10.1080/14733285.2013.743286

Wickham, R. E., & Knee, C. R. (2013). Examining temporal processes in diary studies. *Personality & Social Psychology Bulletin, 39*(9), 1184–1198. doi:10.1177/0146167213490962

Wiles, J. (2011). Reflections on being a recipient of care: Vexing the concept of vulnerability. *Social & Cultural Geography, 12*(6), 573–588. doi:10.1080/14649365.2011.601237

Wiles, R. (2012). *What are qualitative research ethics?* London: Bloomsbury Publishing.

Williamson, I., Leeming, D., Lyttle, S., & Johnson, S. (2012). 'It should be the most natural thing in the world': Exploring first-time mothers' breastfeeding difficulties in the UK using audio-diaries and interviews. *Maternal & Child Nutrition, 8*(4), 434–447. doi:10.1111/j.1740-8709.2011.00328.x

Wiseman, V., Conteh, L., & Matovu, F. (2005). Using diaries to collect data in resource-poor settings: Questions on design and implementation. *Health Policy and Planning, 20*(6), 394–404. doi:10.1093/heapol/czi042

Wolf, M., Chung, C. K., & Kordy, H. (2010). Inpatient treatment to online aftercare: E-mailing themes as a function of therapeutic outcomes. *Psychotherapy Research : Journal of the Society for Psychotherapy Research, 20*(1), 71–85. doi:10.1080/10503300903179799

Worth, N. (2009). Making use of audio diaries in research with young people: Examining narrative, participation, audience. *Sociological Research Online, 14*(4).

Zepeda, L., & Deal, D. (2008). Think before you eat: Photographic food diaries as intervention tools to change dietary decision making and attitudes. *International Journal of Consumer Studies, 32*(6), 692–698. doi:10.1111/j.1470-6431.2008.00725.x

Zhaoyang, R., & Cooper, M. L. (2013). Body satisfaction and couple's daily sexual experience: A dyadic perspective. *Archives of Sexual Behavior, 42*(6), 985–998. doi:10.1007/s10508-013-0082-4

Zimmerman, D., & Wieder, D. (1977). The diary-interview method. *Urban Life, 5*(4), 479–498.

Index

www.ingramcontent.com/pod-product-compliance
Ingram Content Group UK Ltd.
Pitfield, Milton Keynes, MK11 3LW, UK
UKHW020736280225